Through the Valley of Death—Armageddon

More books by John Schroeder

Let Not Your Heart Be Troubled

The Price of Prosperity

God in a Chat Room

Through the Valley of Death
ARMAGEDDON

by John Schroeder

ISBN: 978-0-9843059-0-2

Printed in the U.S.

Acknowledgments

My wife, Stephanie, declined to be listed as the co-author of this book. That does not mean that I don't give her equal credit in writing it. In the same way that it takes two to make a happy marriage, we worked well together in "birthing this baby," of a sort. I provided the ideas and first pass at the text while she worked with those humble beginnings to make it readable as well as entertaining. I am truly blessed to have her love and support through every step it took to complete this book.

There are two people who helped me to enter the world of fictional novels through their skills in editing and offering encouragement. They are Mary Travis and Joanna Schildt.

This is the second book Mary has helped me to publish. Her attention to detail, continuity and context were invaluable in making this story as clean as possible. I can't thank her enough for her service in going above and beyond to help me create this book.

Joanna has been a mentor to me in a number of ways. Most remarkable was her encouraging manner when I decided to start from scratch in rewriting this book. I say that because she had already edited every word of the first draft before I opted to change the focus of the story. She went through each word with me a second time, freely offering her expertise in literature in the areas where I needed her help.

Finally, I want to recognize two people who probably don't know the impact they had on what this book ultimately became. They are Bill Schroeder and Greg Clarke. They are both my brothers; Bill is by blood and Greg is by spirit. The afternoon I spent with them discussing the first draft was what motivated me to start over again. They convinced me to be true to myself rather than settle for a story that was entertaining but did not carry the message I wanted to convey.

To the others who read numerous drafts and offered their feedback, I thank you as well. To list all of you here would be too lengthy, but my appreciation is sincere and I am humbled by the help you have all given so willingly.

Introduction

It is easy to judge a book by its cover but the dynamics of this story cannot be captured by a static image. Some people prefer to read the first chapter or two before passing judgment on a book. While that is usually a fair method of measurement, I would invite you to read through chapter three before thinking you have guessed the plot and conclusion. Then you will have given my efforts a fair trial regarding whether or not you decide to finish the story.

Assuming you do read it to the end, I hope you will not be disappointed to learn that it is the first book in a trilogy that offers a tumultuous ride to a wonderful and brave new world to come. How we ultimately get to that bright tomorrow is a path that you may not have considered. The story only appears to be predictable at first glance. Before the end of book one, you may be surprised at how the best and worst of humankind can combine to build a better world that encourages us to become better people.

I have written a few non-fiction books on the same topics that serve as this story's foundation. While the information in my non-fiction books was well received, I found it was difficult to reach a wider audience if the reader is not entertained during the process. That is why I decided to propose a different world view in a fictional novel format. This book indeed engages your imagination, but it also offers a deeper look at several controversial subjects. It is profoundly optimistic and it describes the world in a way you may not have previously considered.

I am writing Book Two as this one is being published, so you won't have long to wait!

Through the Valley of Death
ARMAGEDDON

Chapter 1

Private First Class Wiley kept the truck's window wide open to let the cool desert breeze kick-start his brain. The coffee cup he kept trading for the gear shift also helped to clear his head. He looked at his watch again and sighed. It was 3:24 am, only three minutes since the last time he'd checked. Wiley knew another hour of unpaved roads lay ahead before they would arrive at the depot. Per regulations, Private Shaw was riding shotgun along with him. Despite the bumpy ride and rules against it, Shaw was fast asleep with his cap pulled down over his eyes.

Wiley looked in his rearview mirror for the headlights of the other "deuce and half" 2½ ton M-35 truck that followed convoy style behind him. Both he and Private First Class Mendez, the other driver, had navigated this hazardous route through northern Israel many times before, but a cargo of high explosives always upped the stakes.

Suddenly, the truck's frame hit the ground hard as Wiley's right front tire bottomed out in a pothole. He quickly recovered control of the truck, but his coffee was a goner. To his amazement, Private Shaw was able to sleep on undisturbed. Wiley kept driving but the pothole really had his adrenaline pumping. He had to remind himself that C-4 is quite stable and wouldn't explode even if the truck had turned over. Then he smiled and wondered which would be worse, the C-4 igniting or his commander's explosive reaction if this load wasn't delivered on schedule. He leaned forward in his seat deciding to keep a closer eye on the road.

These oh-dark-hundred transport missions always put Wiley in a bad mood. He usually made his deliveries to the remote supply depot around 10:00 am, but the Israeli weather forecast for that morning said a heavy storm was due in just after sunrise, and so here he was. He glanced longingly at the spilled coffee on the floorboards and tried to occupy his mind while closely watching the road.

Wiley thought back to his great run of luck the night before. His favorite entertainment was playing cards, and his favorite casino was located in Alumot just southwest of the Sea of Galilee. He was up several hundred when he remembered this early morning mission was only a few hours off. When Wiley said he had to leave because he was scheduled for an early run, the other guys were relieved. He was always a good poker player, but that night he had luck with him as well by winning several hands on the river (the last card drawn) in Texas hold'em poker. Wiley wished now he could trade a few of those winning hands for a good night's sleep.

★★★

Wiley saw something wasn't right about the road perhaps 50 yards in the distance. Instead of the usual tire ruts in the dirt, there was a five-foot section where the road was unusually smooth. He stopped in front of the graded part of the road and shook Private Shaw's shoulder to wake him. Shaw took off his cap and looked around but nothing registered. He was still disoriented and had no idea why they had stopped.

The two-way radio crackled and the voice of Mendez came through from the other truck. He asked what the holdup was. Wiley responded that there was something wrong with the road and to keep an eye out. Mendez started to switch frequencies to call ahead to the depot while his passenger, Private Reynolds, quickly reached for his rifle. It was already too late.

Using the cover of darkness, two men had quietly moved up along the sides of the rear truck and slammed the butts of their rifles through the open windows into the faces of both men. Mendez and Reynolds were out cold when they were pulled from the cab and forcefully thrown to the ground. They were stripped of their Army Combat Uniforms—ACUs— and quietly executed with brutal bayonet jabs.

Unaware of the violence behind him, Private First Class Wiley left his diesel engine running and the headlights on high beams as he stepped out to investigate the smooth patch of road. Private Shaw, still only half awake, grabbed his rifle and begrudgingly slid out of the truck to join Wiley. They both stared at the recently graded dirt and wondered why it was there. The answer became obvious a moment later.

A single rifle shot rang out over the sound of the idling engines. "Don't move!" yelled a threatening voice from behind them. The words were spoken in English, but with a distinctly Arabic accent.

Wiley couldn't believe it. He had heard of terrorist activity within the borders of Israel, but he had never heard of a face-to-face assault on an American military convoy. The significance of this raced through his mind as he automatically put up his hands to show he held no weapons. Private Shaw reluctantly let his rifle fall to the ground. At first, all they could see was the front of their truck surrounded by darkness. Then they saw a man walking toward them silhouetted by the truck's headlights.

Wiley couldn't see the man's face, but he could tell he carried an AK-47 rifle from its outline. The man spoke quickly, but Wiley caught every word despite his thick accent.

"You are now prisoners of war captured by the army of Mohammed's Faithful. If you do everything I say, you may survive this night."

Wiley and Shaw realized this whole thing had been a trap to get them to stop. Feeling a little stupid and very scared, they both knew surviving this ordeal was unlikely.

The hijacker continued, "You two will complete your mission as ordered. You will drive these trucks and my men to the supply compound. We leave now."

He pointed his AK-47 at Wiley and motioned for him to get into the driver's seat. Shaw was pushed from behind toward the second truck. He caught his breath and hesitated when he saw Mendez and Reynolds lying dead on the road. One of the hijackers jabbed at Shaw's ribs with the barrel of his rifle to keep him moving.

Wiley just stared as one of the hijackers handed the man, who was obviously their leader, Mendez's ACU shirt and cap. He kept Wiley at gunpoint while the man in charge put them on. Wiley was filled with dread as he started to piece together their plan. Anyone would assume this hijacker was a soldier in the U.S. Army because he was clean-shaven and wearing a United States military uniform.

Wiley knew he and Shaw were out of options. By the different voices he could tell there were eight or more hijackers. He figured their plan was to infiltrate the supply depot by posing as soldiers riding shotgun while the others stayed hidden in the back of the M-35s. He couldn't see any way to stop them that wouldn't get himself and Shaw killed. Even if they tried and failed, the hijackers would still have the trucks to do whatever they had planned.

The more he thought about it, the more Wiley knew he had to count on the compound's 100 soldiers and security protocols to keep this situation from getting any worse. He knew that once the trucks were in sight of the gate the guards would radio him. Then he was expected to either give the "all-clear" or use the code phrase to signal trouble. Until then, he would do his best to stay alive.

★★★

Colonel Achmed Mansur, Commander of Mohammed's Faithful, heard the report from Hakim on the radio that the trucks had been successfully hijacked without incident. The American hostages were cooperating, so far, and had resumed driving toward the compound. The drivers knew their passengers had hand guns trained on them ready to fire if needed. They were also told that AK-47 rifles were aimed directly at them from the canvas-covered truck beds. Colonel Mansur told his men they had less than an hour to be ready.

★★★

Amon was the best sniper among the 150 soldiers in Mohammed's Faithful. He silently prayed to Allah for help as he anxiously watched the American guards at the front gate of the compound. From his position in the nearby hills, he could see their attention was focused on the two military trucks headed directly for them. One of the guards picked up a radio and Amon was intensely alert. They didn't always do security checks, so the next minute would be critical to the success of their mission.

Setting aside his binoculars, Amon picked up his M-40 sniper rifle. He motioned for his fellow sniper, Abel, to do the same as they made ready to teach these infidels a lesson they would not soon forget. Months of careful planning would be wasted along with the lives of many of Mohammed's Faithful if all did not go well at the gate. If the approaching trucks were not allowed to enter the compound, may Allah guide their aim to see that His will is done.

The real question, Amon knew, was if the drivers would try to take heroic actions once they arrived at the front gate. If so, then it was his and Abel's job to shoot the guards as their fellow soldiers inside the trucks killed the drivers. Assuming it came to that, they might still enter the compound and complete their mission.

★★★

The radio crackled inside Wiley's cab. The gate guard was calling for confirmation that everything was copacetic as the trucks approached. Wiley looked at the man holding the gun and told him that if he didn't respond, the guards would not let the truck enter and would call for backup. The soldier pointed a .45 caliber pistol at Wiley and nodded toward the radio.

"Gate security, this is M-35 leader. We are on final approach and everything is A-OK," said Wiley.

The gate guard asked him to repeat and Wiley did as requested. With a quick "10-4," the soldier signed off and went inside the guard shack. The terrorist riding shotgun inside the cab relaxed, but Amon could see through his scope that the soldier from the gate was making a phone call. The second soldier at the gate took a defensive stance and waited as the truck approached.

As Wiley pulled up to the gate, both soldiers quickly assumed positions at the corners of the truck's front bumper with their M-16 rifles at the ready.

"Are you okay in there Wiley?" the guard who talked to him on the radio asked.

Wiley responded without looking at him, "I told you I was A-OK before and I'm A-OK now."

Just then, a wicked crack whipped through the air that sounded like the sizzle of lightning before the boom. The first guard was falling to the ground when the crackling sound came again. The second guard fell where he stood from the sniper's round fired 500 meters away. The two soldiers in the cabs didn't hesitate and shot both Wiley and Shaw simultaneously. They opened the drivers' doors and pushed the Americans out to take up their positions behind the steering wheels.

Wiley's luck continued to hold. The bullet smashed through his right arm with the humerus bone deflecting its path away from his vital organs. His injuries were limited to a broken arm and a couple of cracked ribs. He would survive this night, but Private Shaw was already gone.

★★★

Amon warned Colonel Mansur that the guard at the gate had probably sounded the alarm to bring help. Mansur ordered Amon to let the truck drivers know and to get ready for the assault. Amon notified Hakim that he had perhaps 60 seconds until American reinforcements arrived. Hakim jammed the truck into first gear and floored the accelerator to smash through the gate.

The concrete barriers just beyond the gate held off his first assault and even the second as he reversed the truck and tried it again. On his third attempt, Basir, the driver of the second truck, pulled up beside him. Pushing together, the barriers tipped over and the M-35s were able to shove them and the mangled gate forward. After forcing the concrete barriers ahead for another 20 feet, they had enough room to maneuver away to do some real damage.

Hakim's mission was to destroy the fuel reserves, but they no longer had the element of surprise. He turned left and headed toward the far west end of the post. He saw Basir turn right to take out the ammunition storage facility located to the east.

★★★

Captain Rob Norton was the Officer in Charge of security during night duty. He was at his desk when the call came in from the front gate that Wiley had given the "A-OK" signal. That was the verbal security code indicating they were in serious trouble. He told his sergeant to sound the general alarm and contact HQ to let them know what was happening. There were only two other soldiers on duty with him and just one Jeep parked outside. Rob knew he couldn't wait for reinforcements. Keeping the M-60 machine gun loaded and firing was a two man job, especially with the Jeep on the move. Captain Norton decided it was better if he drove. He prayed they could get to the gate before all hell broke loose.

As they exited the building, Rob heard the rifle shots and knew they were already too late. The Jeep was still 100 yards out when he spotted four bodies lying on the ground near the guard shack. Then he saw two trucks split up after smashing through the security gate with one of them heading straight for him. According to the delivery schedule, the deuce and half trucks were supposed to be carrying C-4 explosives but he had no idea how many men were inside, nor how heavily they were armed.

Captain Norton's Jeep was equipped with four M-16s, eight extra preloaded magazines for the rifles, and four MK II grenades. The C-4 would not explode if only hit by bullets or shrapnel but the grenades would set it off for sure. Norton knew their best bet for this fight was the Jeep's mounted M-60 machine gun. He gave his men the order to fire and they obliged. The oncoming truck's radiator emitted several clouds of steam as the bullets ripped into it. The windshield shattered as well, but it was unclear if the driver was hit or not. He could have ducked in time below the dashboard and might be driving blind until he passed the Jeep.

The M-35 truck was picking up speed as it passed them, so it was a good bet that the driver had survived. Worse yet, terrorists in the back of the deuce and half started shooting back at the Jeep. Two rounds hit just above the knee of one of Norton's soldiers and his right leg was blasted from his body as he toppled over the side. Norton spared a split-second to glance back at his injured man while the other soldier continued to return fire with the machine gun. The rounds ripped through the truck's metal sides and canvas covering. The pattern of bullet holes was tight enough that the terrorists in back had probably all been hit. Only the dense C-4 itself could have stopped any of the M-60 rounds from killing them all.

The truck turned right and was clearly headed for the fuel depot at the far end of the camp. Norton got on the radio and informed anyone listening that there were two M-35 trucks loose in the compound being driven by enemy forces. He announced his location just behind the truck that was headed for the fuel depot. He warned that the other truck must have a different target, probably the ammunition storage warehouse, and to make sure as hell it was stopped before it got there.

★★★

Now the entire compound was awake and moving quickly. The facility was more or less a half mile square and the majority of the buildings were only one story. From most vantage points in the camp the two M-35 trucks could be seen racing to their explosive destinations with American forces in hot pursuit. The good news was that their heaviest armament was already positioned in front of the fuel depot and the ammunition warehouse. The compound was designed to defend against this scenario though no one expected it to ever happen on an American base inside of Israel's borders.

Hakim was doing his best to keep the truck moving toward their goal. He could see the fuel depot's storage tanks directly ahead. He floored the accelerator, kept his head as low as he could and shouted to the soldiers in the back that they were almost to the target. In an exalted prayer he yelled, "Allahu Akbar!"

Indeed those were his last words.

★★★

The two men on guard duty at the fuel depot could already see the fast-approaching M-35 truck. They were stunned, realizing that this was not a drill. Their training took over as they armed and aimed two LAW-72 rockets at the approaching vehicle. They had heard the trucks were carrying C-4. They also knew that the LAW rockets had enough incendiary force that the C-4 would ignite upon impact. Still, that would be nothing compared to the explosion that would occur if the terrorists reached their intended goal. They fired on the truck the moment they confirmed their range to the target.

Both rockets left a trail of smoke from the M-72 launchers all the way to the approaching deuce and half. The resulting explosion knocked everyone to the ground within 100 yards. A few seconds later it happened again, but this time hell was unleashed from the other side of the base. It seemed the soldiers protecting the ammunition warehouse had also hit the bull's eye. Moments passed with the phantom ringing in everyone's ears as the only sound they heard.

The hush lasted about five seconds until the entire compound realized they had successfully stopped the attack. A cheer started at one end of the camp and spread to the other as the soldiers shouted their relief at having repelled this assault. They had no idea that hijacking the trucks had become a ruse to distract the Americans from the real danger. With 150 heavily armed soldiers of Mohammed's Faithful in perfect position surrounding the compound, the real assault was about to begin.

★★★

Mansur had chosen well to select Amon and Abel as his snipers who would take out the guards at the gate if needed. The primary plan had a reasonable chance of succeeding, but the Colonel considered all contingencies when preparing for battle. His past experience had taught him that, so he was not surprised when only the hijacking went according to plan.

The Americans would never know just how much preparation went into this mission. It started with Mansur knowing when to intercept the trucks. They would have perhaps three hours to organize once word was received of the early morning special delivery. To learn when an early morning shipment was scheduled, Mansur had planted an operative in the poker room of the casino to keep an eye on Wiley. It took more than a month to identify him as a regular driver for the target camp as well as his weakness for gambling on cards. The operative was able to immediately notify Mansur that Wiley had a pre-dawn run to make. They confirmed from other sources that the cargo would be high explosives like C-4 or even Semtex. There was only one route from Wiley's military base to the remote supply compound. All that covert preparation had been just the beginning.

Another challenge was how to get the drivers to stop the trucks without damaging them. Mansur's plan was pure genius it was so simple. They would smooth the tire ruts from the road with just a couple of shovels and rakes. He knew that even at a distance and at night a good driver would spot such a contrasting difference in the dirt and gravel. They would become cautious in case landmines or tire spikes had been concealed there.

The truth was that if the infidel soldiers had ignored the perfectly graded section in the road and kept driving, the hijacking would have turned into a chase. That would have ruined the advantage of surprise because the Americans could radio ahead to the compound. Had that happened, they would have settled for the capture of the trucks' cargo. But the driver had spotted the graded section of road and stopped as they had hoped. Mansur's careful planning assured no one had time to send a radio message to the base. Just as important was that the trucks and their load were in perfect condition.

From there, everything fell apart. The guards at the front gate figured out something was wrong and called for reinforcements. The trucks did not easily clear the concrete barriers at the main gate, which forced them to engage in a bloody firefight all the way to their targets. And then to be within sight of their respective goals only to be abruptly cut down was tragic but not unexpected. Once the hijackers' mission had gone awry, Colonel Mansur's plan shifted to take advantage of the confusion. In fact, he was counting on it.

★★★

The LAW-72 rockets fired from the fuel depot ignited the C-4 cargo causing a tremendous shockwave and fireball. The Jeep, Captain Norton and the soldier firing the M-60 machine gun were blown backward by the fiery explosion just ahead of them. Norton looked around and saw that his man had been crushed underneath the vehicle. Norton was thrown clear, but he was badly burned and he could see the jagged ends of his left shin bone sticking through his calf muscle.

Rob Norton got his hopes up for a brief moment when his fellow soldiers started cheering. He too thought they had successfully stopped the attack. But from the bonfire of the C-4 explosion, he could see that enemy combatants were lining up around the security fence of the camp. He tried to yell out a warning but he couldn't make himself heard.

Rob recognized the finality of these last moments. He would not be going home to his wife and baby boy. All the plans he had made for when this tour was over were about to end. He felt shamefully responsible for failing to repel this attack. Now, neither he nor his brave soldiers would be going home to their families.

Heavy machine gun fire and mortar rounds started exploding throughout the compound. The Americans quickly understood this battle was not over. The enemy had them surrounded and caught with their pants down. Norton watched in helpless anger as a mortar round finished what the hijacked M-35 truck had started, the annihilation of the fuel storage tanks. The tremendous explosion was echoed moments later when he saw and heard the ammunition warehouse being destroyed in the distance.

All Norton could do was pray but he knew it was too late. He couldn't help but think, "Why? What possible motive could these terrorists have for targeting this remote location inside Israel's borders?" Through his agony, he also realized that this could signal the beginning of a war. The U.S. would not take this unprovoked attack lightly.

All those thoughts ceased abruptly when he saw the machine gun's tracer rounds headed his way. One of the bullets savagely ripped through his right side and he knew the end had come. He would bleed out in seconds if nothing else happened to kill him sooner. He tried to picture his wife and son as consciousness faded. His last words were barely audible as he whispered, "I'm so sorry…"

★★★

Colonel Mansur's mission was to destroy the fuel depot and ammunition warehouse with a minimum of casualties to his own troops. Although Hakim's and Basir's men were willing to die to strike this tremendous blow against the American infidels, the primary plan had been for those men to survive.

There was flat desert for 500 meters surrounding the camp that was under constant, automated surveillance. If they attacked by force, his 150 men would be easily detected and wiped out before they could breach the perimeter. Mansur decided the better way to destroy the two targets was by stealth of a few men while using his other troops and firepower to provide cover for their escape. However, the moment the trucks met trouble at the gate, Mansur knew that Hakim, Basir and their people would not survive this mission.

His backup plan was a direct assault on the entire compound using the diversion of the two M-35s to surround it unnoticed. Once his troops had safely reached the security fence, Mansur's men more than completed the mission with brutal and overwhelming firepower. There was nothing left standing inside the compound when Mohammed's Faithful received the signal to cease fire.

The trickiest part of this mission was still ahead of them. That was to move his soldiers and equipment out of harm's way in less than 30 minutes. Months before, a clean escape out of Israel seemed impossible. But Mansur devised a way to pull it off and perhaps make further missions into Israel equally promising.

Their quickest exit from Israel would be the Jordanian border, about seven miles to the east of the supply depot's location. The faster they left Israel, the more likely that re-tasking U.S. satellites and deploying Israeli troops to search for them would fail. An impressive tunnel network had been secretly excavated underneath the Israel/Jordan border over a period of months. The area was uninhabited because it was nothing but sand, dirt and rock. The underground facility Mansur built was large enough to hide his soldiers and their complement of equipment, although they were limited to using Jeeps and trailers that would fit in the tunnels. But those had been enough.

Twenty minutes after their attack on the compound was over, the first vehicles quietly disappeared into the tunnels leading to the Jordanian border. What was left of the original 150 soldiers would stay hidden underground for a few days before returning to civilization in small groups. Their departures would be spread out over time and different exit routes would be used to avoid being of notice. All the equipment and ordinance would remain hidden underground, hopefully ready for the next mission.

Chapter 2

Matthew Alexander fumbled over the objects on his nightstand with confused annoyance. He was only three hours into what he had hoped would be a full night's sleep. As his mind struggled for consciousness, he mistook the second ring of the phone for an alarm clock. By the third ring he had it figured out. He put the handset to his ear and mumbled, "This had better be good!"

"Mr. President?" the nervous voice began. "Mr. President, I am told that you will want to attend a briefing at the White House."

"You've got to be kidding," Matt complained immediately. "We just got to Camp David."

"Mr. President, there's been a terrible attack on an American supply base in Israel," the voice continued. "The National Security Council members are gathering to meet you in the Situation Room as soon as you can join them. Marine One is standing by."

Now Matt was wide awake. "Was this another biological attack?"

"I don't think so, Mr. President. There were few survivors to infect. That's everything I know for sure. Can I tell the White House staff when to expect you?"

Matt hesitated and then asked, "Is Erin, I mean the First Lady, awake yet?"

"I'm not certain, Mr. President. Do you want her notified of the situation?"

"No! Don't tell her what happened, just wake her and give her the option of coming back to the White House if she chooses. I'll be ready to go in fifteen minutes." And with that, Matt hung up and headed for the shower.

★★★

Erin Alexander and Murray were already waiting on board Marine One when Matt climbed the steps into the helicopter. Erin was scratching Murray's ears and he wagged his tail seeing Matt walk in. An aide checked to make sure POTUS (the President of the United States) and FLOTUS (the First Lady) were secured in their seats. Murray also allowed himself to be buckled in with a dignified turn of his head. The aide then signaled to the pilot they were ready to go.

As Marine One lifted off and veered toward the White House, Erin asked, "What is it this time? It had to be bad if they interrupted your vacation plans in the middle of the night."

Matt didn't answer her. He was lost in his own thoughts of how to react to this latest assault. He still didn't know the details, but at least it wasn't another biological strike. Matt wondered if it was a good or bad sign that these escalating attacks had a sudden change in tactics.

Erin asked again in a louder voice, "Matt, can you tell me what's going on?"

Matt couldn't ignore her any longer. "I really can't. I don't know much and I don't know if I can share anything as yet. I'm headed for a briefing with the NSC. I'll know what I can tell you after that."

Erin knew this conversation had ended. She was hardly surprised that he would hesitate to fill her in on what was happening. She typically learned more roaming the halls of the White House and overhearing the staff's casual conversations than she ever got directly from her husband. "How the hell did we wind up like this?" Erin wondered to herself. They used to be best friends and closest confidants. Keeping the First Lady in or out of the information loop was any President's prerogative because there were no official rules on the issue. Matt had clearly made his choice.

She still loved this man but she no longer felt like he was her friend. They used to have so much in common but they'd grown apart as he ascended to his position as the most powerful political leader in the free world. She remembered his charming sense of humor and playful attitude from their early years together. Erin realized that in a very real sense Matt was cheating on her. Not with another woman but with the voters and the media. Erin knew the only occasions when he seemed like his old self were when other people were in the room.

They used to share everything together but that had eroded with each election Matt won and every new state secret he learned. In one sense, she was glad about that. Erin stayed out of politics because she had little patience for making back room deals and voting against one's conscience. Her husband was a masterful politician but what had that cost them as a family? Whenever she made mention of the growing distance, Matt changed the subject or didn't respond at all.

Still, Ronald Reagan was the only divorced U.S. President and his divorce was final long before he took office. Erin had already decided she would make the most of it and continue in her role as a good First Lady. She really wanted what was best for Matt and the country. If she had to put her own happiness on hold for three more years, or even a second term, then so be it. Erin consoled herself with the fact that being the First Lady allowed her to have a greater impact on the people and projects that were important to her.

A short time later, Marine One touched down on the south lawn of the White House. Murray ran on ahead knowing a dog treat would be waiting inside. Matt and Erin also exited the helicopter and, as usual, went their separate ways.

★★★

The pressure felt by everyone in the Situation Room of the White House was intense. Over the past year, American forces had suffered several escalating attacks including two with biological outbreaks persisting after the skirmishes. As with the prior terrorist strikes, there was sparse evidence found to link a militant group or government to the attack in Israel. The major loss of life combined with the previous use of biochemical weapons could not be allowed to go unanswered. If the U.S. response to these attacks was not handled properly, it could mean all-out war in the Middle East.

The only face missing from the members on the NSC committee was the Director of National Drug Control Policy, Gil Kowalski. He was in South America at the moment and not typically involved in military matters unless illegal drugs were involved. General Martin McComb,

Chairman of the Joint Chiefs of Staff (JCOS), was concluding his initial briefing on the horrific massacre in Israel.

The General added, "I hate to admit it, but they've crossed a line this time I never thought they would. I can't imagine what these terrorists believe warranted the annihilation of our supply depot, especially one located inside Israel's borders. I recommend that our response be unmistakably strong to discourage any such future actions against us."

Secretary of Defense Steve Lombard offered a different perspective. "Would a strong response bring them back to reality or perhaps escalate matters? I agree that we can't be seen as indecisive or hesitant in dealing with these continued acts of aggression. However, what can we do now that won't be used as cause to make matters worse?"

The room settled into an uneasy silence. Matthew Alexander looked up to see everyone staring at him waiting to hear his thoughts. He suddenly felt dizzy and began to notice an unusual glow around Steve Lombard. It somehow sparked a daydream of his earlier self. A younger Matt would have considered ways to respond peacefully without appearing weak. He once believed that all conflict could be resolved without violence. That perspective, he knew now, was naïve. A few decades in politics would harden anyone and you couldn't become President of the United States by being naive.

Matt's Chief of Staff, Michael Simons, broke the silence hoping to give his boss more time to consider his options. As Michael calmly recapped where things stood at the moment, Matt was doing his best to focus. He saw the same strange luminescence surrounding Michael that had enveloped Steve Lombard just a minute before. The radiance shifted and it appeared as if there was a figure of a man standing just behind Michael in the strange light.

Matt forced his attention back on the meeting. He was embarrassed that he had allowed his thoughts to wander at this most critical time. Once he refocused on the other people in the room, he found that the luminescence had vanished with the feelings of dizziness. He mentally reviewed his position on the Middle East considering this latest attack.

He felt he could no longer trust several of the Muslim politicians in the Middle East to keep their extreme factions in check. He knew that some

Muslim leaders were good and honorable men. The problem was that the altruistic thinkers among them were few in number and certainly not in control of their governments or people. Matt concluded he had exhausted all reasonable options to achieve peace without violence. Perhaps it was time to take off the gloves and show the terrorists what they were really up against.

President Alexander decided it was time for decisive action. He did not mince words as he set the course for their next steps. "I am leaning toward a response that sends a stronger message than they might expect. We have endured an increasing number of terrorist attacks against our people and allies over the past year. The two biological outbreaks were quickly contained but by any definition they constitute the use of WMDs. While the governments of these countries have declared they want peace, they seem to turn a blind eye to the terrorist factions among their people who continue to attack civilian and military targets. Allowing these groups to organize and train within their borders must be defined as an act of complicity and aggression against America. The action we'll take, once we can confirm who is responsible, should put any government that aids these terrorists on notice that it stops now! So I'm ready to hear what you people think will best send that message."

Secretary of State Joan Hartley was the first to voice her thoughts. "If you're serious about sending a strong message to any government complicit in these attacks, then our response cannot be limited to a surgical strike against the terrorists who annihilated the supply depot. Chances are the people who actually did this have gone in a hundred different directions by now. They know their best defense against our retaliation is to disperse and disappear."

The President thought for a moment before asking, "What do we know of the terrorists' escape? Have we been able to track them? That would certainly help identify our options for a proper response."

General McComb was waiting for this question but he didn't relish answering it. "The moment we received word of the attack, we scrambled our jets. We also re-tasked the satellites covering that area to detect any movement of personnel in the vicinity. The Israelis deployed ground troops but were unable to pick up the trail. Our best guess is that they are still in hiding within a ten-mile radius of ground zero and doing a damn good job of it. We don't believe they could have moved outside of that radius in the time allowed."

Matt looked to George Salazar, Director of the CIA, for his opinion. George nervously cleared his throat knowing he had nothing. "We have few operatives in northern Israel who aren't specifically focused on Syria, Lebanon or various terrorist cells. While many groups have already claimed responsibility for this attack, it seems likely that only someone with the resources of a government or a larger militant group like Hezbollah could have pulled this one off. As usual, the terrorists who didn't do it are the ones who claim the credit. We're working quickly to get a better grip on this. Since our fly-bys and satellites have been unable to track the retreat of the attackers, we are sending investigators to the scene in search of forensic evidence to determine where they went. A heavy storm that already moved through the area has made that search much tougher."

Steve Lombard interjected with a question for the President. "I am certain we will figure out who is behind this. We may be able to tie them to the biological attacks as well, but just how strong a response are you proposing once we identify those involved?"

The room stilled. Matt knew his next words could be the most important of his life. His younger self would have prayed fervently for the answer but he now felt that politics had little to do with God. He had even begun to doubt if God existed in the first place. But that wasn't the question before him. Everyone in the room wanted to know the magnitude of the United States' response.

"Let me be clear," said the President. "They started escalating this conflict by resorting to massive deadly force as well as using WMDs. Therefore, there is nothing in our arsenal that is off the table."

There was no misinterpreting that statement. If Matt didn't have their full attention before, he had it now. "We need to know who is account-able for all the recent terrorist acts. We need to learn where their training bases are as well as the names of their leaders and where they meet. We also need to know where the funding and logistical support for these terrorist activities is coming from. I have no doubt that part of the investigation will lead to militant factions in the Muslim world. But it is time to establish what links exist between the sovereign governments of the Middle Eastern countries and the abominable groups who commit such monstrous acts. If it turns out that one or more of these governments are using these militant groups as their henchmen to hide their involvement, God help them!"

The President stood indicating the meeting was over. The room quickly erupted into side conversations discussing and arguing the implications of what he had just said. Matt knew it was better to let them all chew on it for a while before they regrouped.

He had taken just a few steps when he began to feel dizzy again. He shook it off and kept walking through the door of the Situation Room. He realized that Michael Simons had asked him something but he had not heard the question. Matt couldn't ignore the mounting ache in his left arm coupled with the sensation of a tightening band around his chest. The pain became more intense as he recognized the serious nature of his symptoms.

He turned and said, "Mike, I think you'd better get me to a doctor, now!" Matt managed to sit down in a nearby chair before he slumped forward and fell unconscious to the floor.

Chapter 3

Matthew Alexander was aware he was neither asleep nor awake. He searched his memory for a word until it came to him. He was in the 'hypnagogic' state. He laughed to himself for recalling that word from his college days. He tried to remember where he was supposed to be. How long had he been like this? Why hadn't his assistant prompted him to get ready for his next meeting? And then he remembered the chest pains and collapsing in the chair.

When he opened his eyes, Matt found he was back in the Situation Room, but it was not the same. He vaguely remembered seeing that odd luminescence surrounding his Chief of Staff and Secretary of Defense as they spoke. The entire room now had that same incredible glow.

"Hello! Can anyone hear me?" Matt called out in confusion.

There was no response. In fact, Matt couldn't hear anything. He was surprised at the absence of any sound coming from the overhead lights and wall-mounted video monitors that surrounded him. Matt tried again, "Is anyone here?"

A voice responded but it seemed to come from inside his mind rather than from an outside source. "Of course. Where else would I be?"

Matt spun around trying to locate the person talking to him. He hesitated when he realized his instantaneous 360-degree turn to scan the room should have been physically impossible. Out of frustration he yelled, "Where are you?"

The voice responded, "I am right here with you. Just focus on my words and your eyes will begin to see."

Matt vaguely remembered hearing this voice before. Then something very bright started moving in his peripheral vision. He tried to track the motion but whatever it was moved so quickly he couldn't follow it. In frustration he cried out, "Can you hold still? How can I see you if you keep avoiding me?"

The clear voice, mellowed with humor, chimed, "Now that's an interesting perspective! If you can accept for a moment that it is you who has been avoiding me, you will begin to understand the truth of why you are here."

Matt tried to make sense of the words. He closed his eyes and willed himself to calm down. When he opened them again, the details of the room faded while the strange luminescence formed into a familiar person standing directly in front of him.

The voice was now coming from the man. "Nicely done! It's been a while since you have been able to focus this well. It is good that you have for we have much to discuss."

Matt impatiently asked, "Who are you? Where am I? And what are you talking about?"

Then he suddenly recognized the man. Though the voice was different, the face he saw was his own.

The man replied, "You can call me Amelius. You agreed to this meeting and the agenda long ago. As to where you are, that's a tricky question from a human perspective. Your body is being cared for by three exceptional doctors, and they will see you recover remarkably. Your mind is anywhere you want it to be. Right now, you have chosen to be here with me."

Matt hesitated, trying to take it all in. He couldn't think of anything else, so he asked, "Why do you look like me?"

Amelius answered, "How I appear to you is a combination of both our preferences. Seeing me as yourself is meant to help you relax and have more trust in what I have to say."

"And you say I agreed to this meeting?" Matt asked.

"Yes. Even before you were born we both saw the certainty of this critical juncture once you became the President. You knew you would need encouragement to stay the course and achieve a most extraordinary goal."

"I've already seen and agreed to all these things?" Matt asked, vaguely feeling in his gut it was true. "You make it sound like I was predestined to be President and yet I had some choice in the matter."

"Indeed you did!" said Amelius. "You were chosen by many and you agreed to accept this pivotal role in earth's history, or future, depending on how you look at it. That does not mean pre-destiny ever trumps your free will. Nothing is stronger than free will."

"And so what is it that I already agreed to do?" Matt pressed again.

Amelius smiled and said, "You are in a unique position to channel the best and worst of humanity into a wonderful outcome. You have the desire and ability to make choices where everyone wins instead of trying to take advantage of others' weaknesses and that can change the course of humankind."

Matt was unconvinced. "Exactly what choices are you talking about?"

Suddenly the space around them changed as Matt began to receive his answer. It didn't come in words. He felt like he was living inside of an epic movie as he witnessed the various responses, one after the other, that the United States might choose in retaliation to the recent terrorist attacks. He was shown how each of these scenarios would play out, from the historic changes down to the forgettable differences his choices would bring. A feeling of profound sadness overwhelmed him as the scenes before him slowed and then stopped.

Matt asked, "How am I supposed to know which of those is the right response? Some scenarios lead directly to a world war while others inevitably bring terrible suffering that would likely result in a world war anyway. What difference does it make which way I choose?"

Amelius answered gently, "Indeed those are your choices as things stand at this moment. But you stopped before seeing all of the possibilities. There are opportunities still available to you if you can persevere in patience despite all that may seem to go wrong along the way."

"Show me!" said Matt.

The holographic scenes resumed where they had left off. This time Matt saw that happier outcomes were possible, although unlikely. Regardless of which direction he chose, he saw how difficult it would be to stick with the decisions he would have to make in order to succeed. If he failed, he could just as easily cause a world war instead of prevent one.

"And what if I can't do this?" Matt asked. "You can see that it will create a disastrous conflict with three members of the National Security Council if I change directions now. I have already told them I want to deliver a stronger response than even they expect."

Amelius laughed, "You spoke the truth, but the convincing strength of your response will come from within you rather than from any military aggression. Be not afraid of this. I am with you every step of the way."

"I saw that the scenarios with happier results require a profound commitment from my wife Erin. Why does she have to play a role in all this? You must already know that I keep the challenges in our relationship separate from the challenges I face in running the country."

Amelius answered softly but firmly, "This is very important for you to understand. Repairing your relationship with Erin is as a microcosm of the enormous global task before you. At a later time, another like me will help and guide you in your relationship with Erin."

Despite everything Amelius had just shown him, Matt feared that healing his relationship with Erin was less likely than achieving world peace. His mind was spinning with all he had just experienced. He barely noticed his conscious mind regaining control of his thoughts as he drifted back into a deep sleep.

★★★

The next time he opened his eyes he saw Erin. She stood next to his bed frantically gesturing to the doctors that he was awake. He reached for her hand but realized his whole body was weighed down with wires and tubes. He tried to say something to her, but his voice failed him. He coughed and that finally caught her attention.

"Well, I guess your heart has made you stronger!" she said.

Matt managed to whisper, "What?"

"Isn't that what they say? That which doesn't kill you makes you stronger? The doctors said your heart was beating erratically for three or four minutes."

He mumbled, "So I'm okay now?"

Erin couldn't hold back a guarded laugh. "They say there is no damage to the heart muscle and all your vital signs are good. It was a moving blood clot rather than a full blockage in the arteries that started the episode, but you seem to be out of danger for now. The question of permanent damage is still up in the air because the doctors couldn't tell if your brain was deprived of oxygen. How do you feel?"

Matt finally understood his situation and simply replied, "Tired."

"Well, you've been in bed for the past twenty-four hours when they weren't removing the blood clot or running tests. Still, I'll bet you are tired after all you've been through."

Matt nodded off again remembering the bizarre dream that started with his heart attack. He foggily recalled an extensive briefing with detailed video for each response scenario. Some of it had to do with the recent violence in Israel. Some of it concerned his marriage to Erin. He understood that every bit of the dream was important but, for the life of him, he wasn't sure why.

As Matt went back to sleep, Erin picked up where she'd left off in her book. She took a moment to thank God for bringing her husband back from the brink of death. She prayed that he would make a full recovery while secretly wondering if that would be in the best interests of the nation and the world.

Over the years, their political views had drifted in different directions. They had started out together with closely aligned perspectives on most everything. They wanted to share their vision of an even greater America with the world. Erin watched as Matt's political career skyrocketed by winning election after election. Outwardly, he seemed happy and ever more the personification of "the people's choice." Inwardly, she saw him change from being an altruistic visionary to a cynical pragmatist. She watched as he increasingly traded his vote for agendas he didn't support in order to secure the backing he needed to advance his political agenda and office. And as he pulled away from her politically, she could see that their relationship was coming apart as well.

For a couple of years now, their marriage had existed as just another political convenience. They 'lived in separate rooms' in every sense of the phrase. She was determined not to divorce him while he was active in politics, but their marriage had become a dull shadow of the love and friendship they once felt for each other. Erin had tried to tell Matt he had lost his way by allowing his ambition to become President to justify the means he used to get there. He had snapped back that she simply did not understand. His goal in making all these 'deals with the devil' was to put him in a position where he was beyond anyone's grasp. Once he was elected President, he'd never again agree to anything he didn't truly support.

Erin had tested that promise the day after Matt's inauguration. She overheard him speaking on the phone to a senior Representative from California in an effort to get his proposed legislation passed through Congress. It was the same old story; they promised support for each other's bills even though neither of them believed in the worthiness of the other's legislation. When Erin reminded Matt that he could and should stop compromising his beliefs now that he was finally President, he told her to "stay out of it." And so she had remained distant in body, mind and soul until the heart attack forced her to step up and be a supportive wife in his time of need.

★★★

As Erin remained at Matt's bedside in the ICU, his dreamlike memories of his time with Amelius became clear again. One of the important scenes Matt witnessed was intended to remind him of the love they once shared. He reminisced about the first time they spoke to each other after being paired up on a college science project.

"So are you conservative or liberal?" he asked with a broad smile.

"I'm neither. My name is Erin," she replied coldly.

Matt realized he was so intent on impressing this beautiful woman with his political savvy that he had completely forgotten to introduce himself. He tried to think of something that would help him recover from his botched first impression. The painful silence between them turned to embarrassment.

He finally said, "I was hoping to start over with a witty comeback, but I've got nothing. You're obviously better at this so help a guy out. What can I say now to impress you?"

"I don't think so. It's much more fun to watch you squirm," Erin shot back, appreciating his discomfort and starting to enjoy the exchange.

"Matt Alexander," he said wryly as he offered her his hand.

She took it gracefully and answered, "I know who you are. You've done an annoying yet very effective job of plastering your name and face on every bulletin board across campus. Clearly either politics or marketing is in your future."

"So, can I count on your vote?" he asked with a grin, trying to change the subject over to his comfort zone.

"Seriously? I vote that we stay focused on this class and getting an 'A' on this project." Erin was warming to Matt's charm, but she refused to show it.

He quipped, "So you're a bright lady who never got a 'B' in her life? Lucky me! But what if I'd rather have your vote than an 'A'?"

Erin visibly softened and said, "If you continue to show up, I'll make sure our team gets an 'A.' And just so you know, I don't believe politicians have the answers we need to make a better world."

Hoping he still had a chance with her, Matt asked, "Do you drink coffee, Erin?"

★★★

Matt suddenly flashed forward to the ICU room to see Erin still standing at his side. He found himself floating in the upper corner of the room and realized he was out of his body. He felt great despite his brush with death. Looking down, he heard himself tell her he was "tired" as he closed his eyes to sleep.

He was surprised to find he could clearly read Erin's thoughts as if they were his own. She was reminiscing about the more notable moments of their relationship. Erin remembered how happy they were when they first met in college. Matt winced at the flood of sad emotions that followed her next thoughts. She was regretfully thinking how different her life could have been had she declined that fated cup of coffee.

Chapter 4

President Alexander walked into the Situation Room some nine days after his not-so-graceful exit. The members of the NSC all stood and applauded his return. Matt humbly took his seat visibly touched by the sincerity of their reception. He smiled and got right down to business. "Thank you all for your concern, patience and support over these recent days! Now what have we learned since our last meeting?" he asked with reassuring strength.

CIA Director George Salazar was first up in the briefing. "We sent in ground investigators to collect any forensic evidence that would prove who was behind the attack in Israel. There has been nothing definitive as yet mainly because there has been so much evidence to evaluate. Most of the equipment and weapons used by the terrorists originally came from the United States. It's not unusual for American made weapons to be used against us. However, weapons manufactured in Russia, China and France were also part of the forensic arsenal gathered in trying to prove who was behind the assault.

"We had better luck locating where the attackers had gone after they razed the supply depot. With the help of the Israelis, finding the trail the terrorists took heading east was not difficult. However, the storm that passed through the area within hours of the attack made it almost impossible to determine their final destination." Salazar added, "By now the terrorist troops have likely disbursed and gone to their homes rather than staying together as a military unit."

Secretary of Defense Steve Lombard stepped in to cover Salazar's disappointing lack of progress. "We have satellite intel of increased civilian travelers just over the Jordanian border in the general vicinity of where we think they went. We believe most if not all of the people moving about the area over the past week are mostly made up of the terrorists who attacked the compound. The movement of these pedestrians was meant to appear as if it was random but we have narrowed our search grid because of this unusual foot traffic. A careful evaluation of this area should soon yield results. We are hampered by the likelihood that they were all temporarily sequestered in an underground facility located inside Jordan's border. Knowing now to search for a hideout below ground, it shouldn't be long before we find the entrance tunnels, hopefully on the Israeli side of the border."

President Alexander suggested that diplomatic channels should be used to contact the Jordanian government. They would need permission to conduct a search for the terrorists within Jordan's sectors of the grid once they had proof of their presence. Then he looked at Secretary of State Joan Hartley, and asked, "What is the mood and feeling of the major powers in the Middle East? What do they expect us to do?"

Joan replied, "Your recent health challenges have made everyone nervous. Apparently there were leaks that all options are on the table in responding to these attacks once the culprits and targets are identified. No one wants to make a war out of this but there are many who think violence against our posts in the Middle East will not end until they understand America will no longer tolerate these attacks. Vice President Jefferson calmed the waters while you were in recovery but now the world is waiting to hear directly from you."

Matt went on record, "Eric, I want to thank you for the outstanding job you've done over these past days. I can't imagine where we'd be now if you had not kept such a steady hand on things while I was getting back on my feet." The Vice President blushed a bit at the praise and nodded his acceptance. Matt continued, "This may sound odd, but in some ways the timing of my episode could not have been better. It gave me and the government leaders involved a chance to let our fears fade and tempers cool. I'm almost relieved to learn that my willingness to leave all options open regarding our retaliation was leaked. No doubt hearing that raised the stakes but it also has everyone thinking this has gone too far. So now, General McComb, what do you suggest we do in response?"

The JCOS Chairman instantly felt the weight of the world on his shoulders. "Our best guess from what we know now is that an extremist group of trained terrorists known as Mohammed's Faithful was responsible for this heinous attack. Despite the probable underground bunker that made possible the terrorists' escape, we don't believe the Jordanian government was involved. The area in question is fairly close to the Syrian and Lebanese borders. So it is possible either of their governments could have been helping Mohammed's Faithful in the attack and to escape undetected. We have yet to conclusively prove any of this, but if we need a 'best guess scenario' to bounce around, a partnership between Syria and a militant faction of between 100 to 250 soldiers is a reasonable start."

Matt asked, "Are there any other governments besides Syria, Lebanon or Jordan who could have been involved in this?"

McComb answered, "That's still hard to say. We haven't been able to rule any of them out but the one with the most to gain and least to lose over this seems to be Syria so far."

"Is there a name for the region where our supply depot was situated? I've seen its location on the briefing maps, but what's the nearest city or landmark that a tourist would recognize?" Matt said looking at the video monitor with a map of the region.

McComb hesitated but then answered, "As you can see, there are no nearby cities or towns. We purposefully choose our supply locations to remain out of the spotlight while still being accessible by air and ground. The compound itself was on the east end of Israel's infamous Jezreel Valley."

Matt had to ask, "Why do you say infamous? I've been to Israel a few times and I don't remember much being said about the Jezreel Valley."

General Martin McComb took off his glasses and wiped them as he tried to look casual. "The Jezreel Valley's modern name is neither well-known nor infamous, really. However, in biblical times it was called Armageddon."

The people in the room collectively held their breath. The history of that name and place was known to all. President Alexander attempted to break the tension by saying, "Then let's see what we can do to make the best of what happened in the Jezreel Valley rather than using it as an excuse to fulfill an ancient doomsday prophecy!"

There was an excited reaction to Matt's revised directive. They were largely relieved that WMDs weren't automatically included in the response scenario. There were also a few in the room who were not pleased with this development. They were tired of terrorists and fanatics taking advantage of the United States' endless forgiveness born of a desire for peace. They believed that "peace was possible through force" if key groups were eliminated leaving only the right people in charge of the Holy Land.

★★★

Today had been one of the most frustrating days General McComb could remember. He thought the President was about to give the green light to shut down terrorism once and for all in the Middle East. He couldn't understand what changed his mind. He had no idea why the President was wavering, but McComb knew in his heart the country couldn't afford to let this perfect opportunity pass.

He poured a tall drink of single-malt scotch and sat back in his oversized easy chair to assess the situation. McComb knew that Director of National Intelligence Rick Newman agreed the time to strike was now. By the look on CIA Director George Salazar's face at today's meeting, he was probably the angriest guy in the room when POTUS set a new direction for their response strategy. McComb decided he would arrange to meet with Newman and Salazar. He was sure that together they could steer things back in the right direction. McComb drifted off to sleep reviewing their options.

As his subconscious mind took over, he was soon dreaming. Martin first sensed he was weightless and then he took off like a rocket. He looked around and couldn't make sense of his surroundings. He felt like a bubble floating up from the bottom of the ocean but he wasn't wet despite the sensation of rushing water. He then catapulted out of the stream landing abruptly without feeling the impact.

Martin found himself in a nondescript room with three other people. He recognized two of the men, Rick Newman and George Salazar, but the third man was unknown to him. There was an intense glow to the man's presence that made him appear to be dressed completely in white.

The unknown man was the first to speak, "Welcome! My name is Halaliel. The important events of today have brought us together to discuss the critical choices before you."

George Salazar responded, "You said your name is 'Ha lay lee al? Uh, okay. And what do you know about today's events?"

McComb and Newman were just as confused as Salazar.

Halaliel smiled and said, "My name is as unique as it is ancient. As to what I know about the President's NSC meeting, well, there's very little I don't know."

All three mumbled their objections, but Halaliel held up his hand and added such an authoritative look that they all fell silent. "You three are in the dream state together and this place is apart from the earthly realm you call home. Your minds often travel away from your body while sleeping but you rarely remember what occurs. That's because your conscious mind can't remember what it doesn't understand. Instead, you often wake remembering what happened as if it were just a dream. While correctly interpreting dreams can reveal the guidance contained in the symbolism, those messages are easily ignored in the waking state."

Salazar couldn't help but ask, "If we won't remember what you're about to say, why are we here?"

Halaliel smiled and said, "I personally feel this meeting will change nothing. Allowing your conscious mind to be directed by the subconscious requires a willingness to listen to your inner guidance. The three of you, in your waking state, are so threatened by your perceived enemies that you quit listening to the unobtrusive voice of your subconscious long ago. However, in the surprising event that you take my advice to heart, it will save you and the world much suffering.

You already know that the President is about to reveal an extraordinary response to the attacks against your country. I suggest you three support it to the best of your abilities."

Newman and McComb asked the same question, "What, exactly, is he planning to do?"

"The details are not yet defined because much is still undecided by your President. However, it will not be the aggressive response you had hoped for," Halaliel confided.

Salazar angrily said, "And so you are suggesting we stand by and let these terrorists do anything they want to us when we can so easily wipe them off the face of the earth? What kind of message will that response send?"

"That violence only returns violence and so it must cease. How that cycle is broken depends a great deal on the three of you," he warned with a bit of a challenge in his tone.

They listened as Halaliel explained the possible choices and outcomes they would soon face. When they awoke the next morning, each man vaguely remembered having disturbing dreams. No matter, with the morning's first cup of coffee and a look at the headlines, the dreams were soon forgotten.

Chapter 5

Special Agent Ross was in charge of the team of CIA operatives tasked to track the terrorist soldiers' escape. It was nighttime and progress had been painfully slow because of the storm that moved through the area shortly after the strike. Even though surveillance planes and a satellite search had begun within thirty minutes of the attack, the terrorists' exit plans remained a mystery. That was why the CIA agents were spending most of their time at the Israel/Jordan border nearest the supply depot's location. It was the most likely exit point from Israel given that they had so little time to disappear. It simply would have been impossible for the terrorists to have made it to the border of Syria or Lebanon without being seen in the time it would have taken them to get that far.

Two hundred miles above the earth, a KH "Keyhole" imaging satellite relayed pictures to Ross and his team via the National Reconnaissance Office - NRO - headquartered in Chantilly, Virginia. This particular satellite had been in orbit for thirty years but could still identify objects as small as five square inches at ground level. There was also cutting edge technology assisting in the search. A highly classified satellite telescope developed by Boeing had been tasked to relay images from beneath ground level.

This process requires a helicopter with a shielded X-ray generator installed between its landing struts. It uses technology similar to "painting" a target with a local laser to accurately guide a missile attack. Ross' helicopter team could paint a twenty foot by twenty foot area of land when flying forty to fifty feet overhead. The reflected X-rays from underground allow the Boeing satellite above to 'see' up to fifteen meters beneath the surface, depending on the density of the soil.

Trying to find a tunnel entrance hidden among the many hills and valleys in this terrain was like searching for the proverbial needle in a haystack, but Ross was sure it was only a matter of time until they found it. He knew the tunnel had to be there and they had already covered seventy-five percent of the search grid's sectors. With the increased pressure he was receiving from CIA headquarters in Langley, Virginia, Agent Ross hoped this would be the day he could deliver.

Special Agent Culver called Ross on the radio. He had located numerous faint tire tracks still visible despite the recent storm. Ross contained his excitement, knowing this had happened many times over the past few days with no luck in finding the terrorists. Culver asked for X-ray satellite support of the area. Ross ordered the helicopter to Culver's location and told the pilot to stand by for orders to paint the area. Then he instructed the support team at NRO to focus the Boeing satellite's telescope on the same coordinates Agent Culver had just given. When both teams were ready, he gave the go-ahead to proceed. A minute later the images began to appear on Ross' laptop.

He had received many such scans over the past several days and by now he had a good deal of experience identifying the natural underground terrain. Then he saw it. The green still-shots on his laptop showed an underground passageway close to the tire tracks. Once they located any section of the underground passage, pinpointing the elusive entrance to the tunnel was easy.

The team at the NRO asked him to guide the helicopter along the tunnel's coordinates to find the entrance. The pilot reminded Ross that a complete scan would require that they enter Jordanian air space. Ross gave him the approval to proceed knowing their people had already cleared that through the proper channels. The Jordanian government had been only too happy to demonstrate their cooperation, especially since the terrorists' assumed exit through their border implied they were involved in the attack.

The images continued to update on Ross' laptop and he could see that the other end of the tunnel emptied into a much larger room, still completely below the surface. In fact, the room was so large that the twenty foot by twenty foot X-ray pictures showed only a small portion of the underground chamber. He was able to make out many of the vehicles and trailers parked inside to confirm they had found the right place.

While his laptop connection could only handle downloading still images, the NRO was receiving real-time video. They informed Ross that the subterranean room and tunnels appeared to be abandoned, though it would take hours of careful scanning to be sure. He told them that searching the premises for any stragglers could wait. The priority was the find the entrance and gain access to the underground chamber.

★★★

It was just after midnight in Israel marking the tenth day since the terrorist attack on the U.S. supply depot. Agent Ross was frustrated that he was still unable to provide any answers. However, the time spent searching had not been wasted. The backhoe they'd requested was now on site along with construction work lights and a generator to dig at night. That was exactly what Ross needed to avoid further delays. The backhoe quickly disposed of the camouflaged wall that had completely sealed the entrance to the tunnel leading to the underground complex. He then sent in three two-man teams to recon the area and hopefully capture any terrorists who might still be there.

The main access tunnel had been dug to follow the path of least resistance around naturally occurring boulders. The twisting passageway was perhaps 250 yards long compared to the 120-yard straight shot from the entrance to the large underground room. They knew to watch for booby-traps at all points in and around the area. That made progress slow but no one minded being careful considering the risk.

It would probably take them forty-five minutes to be sure the tunnel was safe all the way to the large chamber. Ross surmised the only reason these vehicles were still there was because the fanatics couldn't remove or destroy them and remain undetected. That made the odds of this complex being wired to blow somewhere near 100 percent. He knew he had the best trained men in the world for this job. They just had to be careful to make sure they got what they came for without casualties to the team.

★★★

Sadad was struggling through his third day of solitude in the underground bunker. Everyone else had already left the hideout and headed for their homes. He was the last remaining soldier of Mohammed's Faithful who had volunteered to keep watch over the weapons and vehicles stored there. He thanked Allah that even though this was perhaps the loneliest mission imaginable, at least it was not designed to end with his suicide. He volunteered after Colonel Mansur assured him that he could fulfill this important assignment and still safely return home to his family.

The entire chamber had been set with explosives, as had the vent shafts leading to the surface. These vents allowed the vehicles to run for brief periods without suffocating the soldiers, as long as they wore gas masks. Sadad's job was to remain in the underground complex for up to two weeks keeping watch for intruders. If the Americans and Israelis had not found their hidden location by that time, they likely never would and all that equipment could be used again someday. If they did manage to find the hidden chamber, it was Sadad's job to detonate the explosives and bury the equipment and infidels under tons of dirt and rock.

He remembered his exact instructions in case this place was discovered. "When the infidels are within 20 meters of the chamber, start the laptop's three-minute countdown that will detonate the explosives. Once activated, the timer cannot be turned off but the infidels won't know that. There is a ladder installed in the nearby ventilation shaft so you can escape on foot leaving the intruders behind to die."

He was perfectly vigilant during the first two days of his mission. He barely slept and had set the laptop computer to emit a tone every thirty minutes to remind him to check the area. Colonel Mansur had told him it would take longer than those thirty-minute intervals for any intruders to enter the chamber. He knew they were trained to check for trip wires and buried mines in the winding tunnel. If Sadad obeyed his instructions, he would soon be home with his family knowing he had served Allah well in their fight against the infidels. However, that intensity of vigilance was difficult to maintain and the hours of solitude in that dark underground chamber took their toll. He began to deviate from his instructions in self-defense of his sanity.

The camera at the opening of the Israeli tunnel was remotely connected to the laptop. He would be able to see anyone coming if they breached the camouflaged wall blocking the entrance to the complex. He didn't have a camera in the other tunnels leading to Jordan, but the odds were negligible that any of the infidels would enter from the Jordanian side. Since there were no lights in the walled-up tunnel, all Sadad could see on the monitor was a dark screen. However, if the wall blocking the entrance was breached, the camera was light-sensitive enough to show that intruders were coming, even at night. He had more than enough charged batteries to last two weeks and the laptop had been modified to allow him to change batteries without having to reboot the computer.

Sadad's first departure from his orders was to use the computer for spiritual enlightenment rather than security. He tried watching religious videos that were stored on the hard drive but he quickly tired of those and moved on to read the Qur'an and a little of Riyad al-Sâlihîn, the most revered Islamic holy books. They too did not hold his attention for long, so he started playing variations of the card game solitaire. Being a good Muslim, Sadad avoided any gambling games that were considered to be makruh, because gambling is sinful according to Sharia law. He found he enjoyed playing a solitaire game called free cell. As he continually tried to improve his score in the game, he became less diligent in checking the camera for signs of intruders. His need to keep himself entertained after this long period of isolation in the dark was the flaw in Colonel Mansur's otherwise excellent plan.

It was a little after midnight and Sadad had been playing free cell for hours. The ongoing music programmed into the computer game had become quite annoying. He was not good with computers so he felt a little pride when he clicked on something that made the music stop. What he didn't realize was he had also muted the regular alarm beeps to wake him from his short naps.

★★★

Agent Ross' backhoe team had just breached the walled-up tunnel entrance. Sadad was sleeping soundly as the special agents quietly moved in to clear any explosives. Almost immediately, they found the camera monitoring the tunnel's entrance. They determined it was strictly for local use but they could only guess if anyone was watching. They destroyed the camera and moved on with the assumption that anyone inside now knew they were coming.

Almost forty minutes after the CIA teams had begun clearing the tunnel, Sadad woke up with a start. He saw the laptop screen patiently waiting for him to resume the card game. He realized he had slept far too long and immediately switched the monitor from the game to the tunnel camera. The screen was dark, as usual, but it didn't look the same as it had before. There were some English words displayed on the monitor that he had not seen before. The laptop was programmed for the Arabic language, but the camera's monitoring software was not designed to tie into the operating system's translation software. The words said, "No Input Signal." Sadad didn't know for sure what those words meant, but he feared the worst.

Grabbing his AK-47 rifle, he moved quickly toward the tunnel on Israel's side of the large chamber. He needed to be sure intruders had come before he activated the detonation timer. To set it off unnecessarily would only alert his enemy where to search and they would probably catch him escaping in the process. He mentally reviewed each step of the plan. He would activate the timer from the laptop computer. He would keep the laptop where the infidels were sure to find it. Then he would escape up the ladder to the surface.

Mansur was sure the infidels would expect the underground chamber to be wired with explosives. Although the detonation timer could not be turned off, Mansur had installed a second software program to confuse them. The computer screen would show a timer counting down as well as an icon labeled 'Abort.' Clicking on the icon would stop the timer on the laptop's display but do nothing to stop the total destruction of the chamber and tunnels.

Colonel Mansur made Sadad repeat how important it was that the infidels immediately find the laptop after starting the countdown. The ruse would give Sadad time to escape. However, if the laptop survived the destruction, the enemy might be able to use it to connect Mohammed's Faithful to other attacks on American targets. The Colonel was angry that his personal laptop was the only one that had both the hardware and software to fulfill this mission. He regretted having to give it up for the cause. Sadad assured Mansur he would do his job and that the laptop would be demolished one way or another.

★★★

Special Agent Ross was near the tunnel entrance following his teams' progress as they cleared the way. He was still calculating the implications of the remote camera they found just inside the concealment wall. Their X-ray satellite intel indicated no people were moving inside the underground chamber. He knew that was not a certainty, but the more time that passed without any signs of life from within, the better he felt. The agents were using night vision goggles (NVGs) rather than flashlights. They were working well and Ross heard the lead team confirm that they could see some vehicles off in the distance.

★★★

Agent Culver was in charge of the lead team that had first entered the tunnel. He rounded the last bend in the path and peered through his NVGs into the gloom ahead. He saw a faint light revealing an underground chamber filled with vehicles. He radioed for everyone to hold their positions and maintain silence while he verified the source of the light. As he watched, the shadows danced around revealing that the light source was moving. In fact, the shifting silhouettes indicated that there were two probable light sources. One was fixed while the second light source was probably a flashlight held by someone moving about in the chamber. Culver determined that the person inside would be far away by now if any of the remaining tunnel was booby-trapped. He decided to act immediately.

He dove headlong into the chamber and rolled to an upright position behind a nearby Jeep. He looked toward the lights and realized he had been right. On a small table about fifty feet off to his left was a TV or computer monitor providing a steady blueish glow. Culver briefly saw the flashlight resting on a table just before his view was blocked by a man taking a seat in front of the screen. Soon he heard the tapping sounds of a keyboard filling the room.

Culver understood that whatever the other man was typing was more important to him than escaping with his life. That made his next move more logical than suicidal. He charged directly for the silhouette as he raised his M-5 rifle to fire. Suddenly, the light from the monitor and the flashlight were gone. Agent Culver fired a three-round burst into the darkness. He could still hear the man's feet scrambling on the floor which meant he had probably missed. Culver slowed but continued to move cautiously forward as his eyes and NVGs readjusted to the darkness.

He covered enough ground to reach the small table where the man had been a moment before. There was an AK-47 lying on the floor and a laptop sitting on the table with the lid closed. Culver looked around for the other man. He saw him sitting motionless with his back to the excavated wall of the cave. He understood that the faint green glow from his NVGs was probably the only thing the man could see.

He was unsure if the man had used the computer to call for help or to set off a bomb, but waiting to find out was not an option. He pulled out an M-84 stun grenade. He yanked the pin and yelled "FLASH BANG" as loud as he could and threw it directly at the seated man. The other agents within earshot would know to cover their eyes and ears to avoid being disoriented by the brilliant flash and gigantic "BOOM" that shook the chamber.

Culver reset his NVGs and looked around. He saw that the man was now lying on the floor clearly bewildered and shaking his head to clear it. Culver took a moment to open the laptop to see what the man had been doing. The screen showed a timer counting down with less than three minutes remaining and his heart nearly jumped out of his chest. Just beneath the timer was an icon with a large typed word in both English and Arabic. The icon read, 'Abort.'

Culver radioed to Ross what he'd found and urged everyone under-ground to evacuate immediately. Ross made Culver's suggestion an order and the men quickly retreated toward the tunnel entrance. Having nothing to lose, Culver clicked on the abort icon and the timer stopped counting down with 2:07 left to go.

★★★

Sadad had never been so scared in his life. He had faced death in battle before, but he had never felt as alone as he did right then. Having dis-covered the intruders were mere meters from entering the main chamber, Sadad knew he had only seconds to set the timer and escape through the ventilation shaft. He barely managed to start the countdown before the first of the intruders fired at him. Sadad had closed the laptop and turned off his flashlight in time to keep from being an easy target. In the pitch black of the huge cave, Sadad blindly crawled on the ground until he bumped into the excavated wall. He couldn't tell if the exit ventilation shaft was to his left or right. He assumed the American soldier would have expensive technology to see in the dark so he decided his best defense was to not move at all.

As his eyes adjusted to the darkness, Sadad could barely see a green light outlining the soldier's head in the distance. He seemed to be scanning the chamber trying to locate Sadad's position. He wasn't sure if the soldier could see him or not, so Sadad held completely still. Suddenly, the green glow moved and Sadad heard something hit the floor of the cave in front of him. Then the soldier shouted something he didn't understand. A second later a painful flash of light and concussive explosion knocked Sadad over nearly causing him to pass out. After a moment, he realized he was only dazed rather than injured.

As he regained his bearings, Sadad observed that the soldier had the laptop open and was speaking on his radio. The faint light from the monitor allowed Sadad to locate the exit ladder to his right. He knew he had to kill this American if there was any chance of escape. He had lost his rifle in all the confusion but he still carried a Russian F-1 hand grenade on his belt. Despite the danger to himself, he decided to use the grenade knowing he would either escape or die heroically.

Sadad pulled the pin and tried to toss the grenade directly at the American. He was still so disoriented that his aim was off by perhaps five meters. However, when it comes to hand grenades, accuracy is not crucial. The soldier dove for cover the moment it hit the ground.

Sadad rushed for the ladder. The grenade's shrapnel would kill him just as easily as it would his intended victim. He prayed that the laptop would be smashed beyond recognition because he wasn't stopping for anything. As he climbed the rungs of the ladder, he counted the seconds expecting the grenade to kill them both at any moment. He got to ten before realizing his escape plan was working better than he had hoped. The F-1 was so obsolete and depleted that it wouldn't have exploded any time in the last decade. His unintended deception of the defective grenade had saved his life but that meant the soldier was still alive as well.

Sadad climbed the last few steps up the ladder and cleared the vent shaft. The sun was not up yet but he could see bright lights off to the west. They were probably the work lights the soldiers used to breach the tunnel's entrance. He had no idea how much time remained before the chamber and access tunnels were destroyed, but he knew he did not want to be standing on top of them when that happened. He set a fix from the North Star toward Syria hoping to get out of sight before the soldier below caught up to him.

★★★

Agent Culver was sure his life was over. He watched as the terrorist threw a hand grenade in his general direction. He knew the thing would explode in seconds and automatically dove to the ground. He curled up in the fetal position and was on his third or fourth "Oh My God!" before he realized nothing had happened. The grenade was a dud. Feeling a little foolish now, Culver stood up as he reset his NVGs once again. He saw the man's legs ascending a ladder up one of the vent shafts. Culver grabbed the laptop and shoved it in his backpack before following the terrorist. "I'm in pursuit of a suspect up a vertical shaft!" he yelled into his radio.

As he reached the surface, the light of the stars would have been more than enough to see through his NVGs. However, the distant glow from the work lights at the tunnel entrance made for easy viewing all around. From the way he was moving, Culver could tell the other man was still disoriented from the flash bang grenade.

He yelled, "HALT!" to the fleeing man and fired a warning shot. It came much closer than he had intended as it ricocheted between the man's feet. The man stopped running and held up his hands in the universal gesture of surrender. Agent Culver radioed to Ross that he had a prisoner in his sights on the surface approximately 300 yards northeast of the tunnel's entrance. He requested backup and added that he could not be sure there weren't more enemy personnel below. Culver slowly approached the man who had just tried to kill him. He directed the man to get on his knees in English. The man didn't comply. Culver heard him speaking in Arabic as he drew closer.

★★★

Sadad knew this was the end of both him and the soldier. He would not survive this mission but he hoped that he had succeeded in doing Allah's will. There couldn't be more than a minute left before the explosives below killed him and the infidel who was probably about to shoot him regardless. Sadad felt like he had failed his family and Colonel Mansur. Why hadn't he done what he was told? He let his boredom and laziness get the better of him and now he would have to pay for that with his life. He heard the soldier yelling to him in English and all Sadad could do in return was to pray aloud. He began with the standing raka'ah prayer of the Salah. He hesitated to go on to the second prayer. That would require him to bow as he recited the words. Instead, he looked at the approaching soldier and defiantly uttered, "Allahu Akbar!"

A moment later the timer expired and so did the underground network beneath them. The U.S. satellite imagery captured the initial explosion and subsequent implosion of earth as the chamber and tunnels breathed out and then collapsed. The few agents who were still below died quickly under the weight of the earth crashing down upon them. Others were incinerated by the blast that pushed through the tunnels and vent shafts with the force of a flame thrower shooting fire more than 100 feet into the dark night. Both Agent Culver and Sadad lost their footing as the ground shifted like quicksand. The earth beneath them roared and collapsed as the dirt, rocks and boulders remixed to form a new foundation below. When the ground stopped shaking and the desert was quiet once again, Agent Culver and Sadad were both badly injured and trapped in the crushing debris.

Sadad could neither move nor breathe. He could only watch as Culver mustered the strength to pull his backpack up through the dirt. He wanted to ensure that the laptop would not be ignored when he was found. The breathing room he gained by removing his backpack served to keep him alive until help arrived. The last thing Sadad saw was the laptop spilling out of the backpack that was now next to the soldier's face. Sadad knew he had failed because both the infidel and that cursed computer would survive this ordeal to reveal their secrets.

Chapter 6

The NSC meeting in the Situation Room was interrupted by an aide with a written message for the President. They had just resumed discussions regarding their response to the attack on the compound in Israel when the intel they had been waiting for finally arrived. President Alexander handed the note to George Salazar and announced the briefing would continue in 5 minutes with an update from Director Salazar. After all, it was his CIA agents who tracked down the evidence and the location of the bunker where over 100 terrorists had hidden and dispersed without detection.

The members of the NSC received identical dossiers containing photos and a synopsis of the evidence collected thus far. George was on the phone with Special Agent Ross who despite his injuries was able to bring them up to speed on the investigation that continued on site. Within minutes, Director Salazar and the other members of the NSC were ready to continue the discussion.

George cleared his throat and read aloud the summary he had just received from Agent Ross. "This morning at approximately 1:00 am local time in Israel, Agent Ross and a team of CIA special agents discovered what they believed could be the entrance to an underground bunker. Their mission was to locate the terrorists who annihilated our Jezreel Valley supply depot seven miles west of the Jordanian border. With the permission of Jordan's government, Agent Ross' men breached the camouflaged tunnel entrance and proceeded to investigate the underground complex. Apparently the terrorists had already evacuated the bunker except for one. Had our people not found this underground location, it is certain the equipment would have been used again by the terrorists at a future date.

"At around 1:45 am local Israel time, the lone insurgent activated a det-onation timer and attempted to escape to the surface before the resulting explosion. An agent was able to recover a laptop computer probably used to facilitate the destruction of the complex. Unfortunately, the resulting explosion killed the man we believe was responsible for destroying the bunker. All of the injured were transported by air to a nearby medical facility in Nazareth. The laptop is already being couriered to Langley where a forensics team will determine if they can recover any incrimi-nating evidence."

President Alexander asked if this meant they were any closer to identi-fying with certainty those responsible for the attack on the supply depot. He could tell that his inquiry had deflated George's enthusiasm, which in itself was an answer.

"Mr. President," he replied, "we don't yet know the answer to that question. However, I am confident that from the physical evidence already recovered and the intel we'll glean from the laptop, we will soon know who was responsible. I can add that nothing we've found so far negates our working scenario that the group known as Mohammed's Faithful is responsible for the attack."

Vice President Eric Jefferson commented, "We initially discussed that there may be Syrian support for the terrorist activities of Mohammed's Faithful. However, I thought all the violent factions moved elsewhere once the Syrian government became unfriendly toward them. In light of that, what makes you believe the Syrian government is helping Mohammed's Faithful?"

Secretary of Defense Steve Lombard responded. "You are correct that Syria's government has taken steps to improve its reputation with the non-Muslim world. Distancing themselves from terrorist organizations and officially inviting them to leave the country allowed for an easing of international sanctions and increased foreign aid that was desperately needed to quell the civil unrest among their citizens. However, it's thought by many that those outward changes were better described as 'cosmetic' to achieve a goal rather than indicating an authentic position against terrorism. Syria, along with Lebanon, still has major issues with Israel over territorial disputes concerning the Golan Heights. They like it when militant factions torment their enemies. In those cases, the Syrian government looks the other way and even offers certain groups whatever support they need."

Eric then asked, "Do we really believe that the Syrian government would risk the gains they've made to help destroy our supply depot in Israel? Where is the advantage in taking that chance?"

Steve conceded that was a good point but the answer required an understanding of their history. "The war with Israel in 1967 is still being waged in the minds of many who fought and were defeated. Some of those angry young soldiers have become the military leaders of those same embarrassed countries. For them, what we call the 'Six Day War' of 1967 was only one battle in a war that is ongoing.

"Syria continues to be quite aggressive and outspoken in their loathing of Israel. They would love to see the U.S. withdraw military support from the Jews. If they can frustrate us enough to reduce or even abandon our military presence in the Middle East, then Syria, Lebanon, Iran and others could organize together and really give Israel a run for their money."

Matt added, "So we may well have government backing of terrorist activities in this case." He turned to General McComb and asked, "In light of these developments, what is the recommendation from our military leaders as an appropriate response to the attacks on our bases in the Middle East?"

As Martin began to outline a series of retaliatory strikes aimed at isolating the perpetrators, Matt found himself mentally drifting away from the subject at hand. He wasn't tired and he'd been off all medications except blood thinners for a few days now. He found himself again reliving the experience after his heart attack. He had not been able to fully recall what happened that day, but he knew what he'd been shown was very important to the decision he was about to make.

While his gaze was fixed on General McComb, Matt remembered he had attended some kind of briefing with just one other person. That unusual man patiently showed him the long history of Middle Eastern conflicts. The 3-D scenes he witnessed went well beyond the images he was used to seeing in a briefing. Strangely enough, he found he was able to feel the emotions of every person affected by thousands of years of war and unrest. He could sense the distrust, the anger, even the hate on both sides of every conflict. It wasn't just the ongoing struggle between the Jews and the Muslims he experienced. He came to realize that kind of negativity was part of every religious and political conflict in the history of the world. To personally feel the suffering of each individual on the planet was overwhelming. It was also quite compelling that something had to be done to resolve it.

Matt pondered what he was told during that odd encounter. He was beginning to think it might have been a near-death experience or NDE. However, he'd never heard of anything like what he'd been through. He wasn't shown the wonders of heaven or deceased relatives from his past. The focus of his NDE, if that's what it was, seemed to be on what he could do now to make things better in the future.

The stranger who had briefed him agreed achieving a peace-loving world was a near-impossible goal as things stood today. He had explained that while most everyone agrees that peace among all nations is preferred, many harbor a deep-seated desire for vengeance because of the sins committed against them and their people. He had also suggested this was because humankind has little faith in the righteousness of outsiders. For thousands of years all conflicts in the Middle East could be summed up as 'us against them.'

From this new and unusual perspective, Matt began to see that violent solutions only attracts more violence. Each transgression only amplifies our desire for vengeance and that helps us believe we are ridding the world of evil. Such a vicious cycle, because it feeds itself, can last forever.

Matt realized General McComb had stopped talking and all eyes were on him. They thought he was shaking his head to McComb's proposed response scenarios. Their worried expressions conveyed concern that he might still be recovering from his health challenges regardless of his doctors' consent that he could return to work. No one knew what to say, so they awkwardly waited as they stared.

Matt decided to plunge right in with his revelations by posing a question. "Is there any response we can agree upon among ourselves that would be so clearly appropriate that everyone in the world would agree we've done the right thing?" The members of the NSC looked at each other as they silently wondered where POTUS' question was leading.

"If we were able to conduct a strike where only those responsible for the attacks against us were killed, would there be 100 percent agreement around the world that our response was correct?" Matt paused for effect and then continued, "I think it is safe to say that whatever 'appropriate response' we come up with, there will be those who think we have no right to retaliate. Others will feel we didn't go far enough. But either way, the conflict will continue as before and the violence will probably escalate. If no correct 'appropriate response' exists, then what can we do that will make things better?"

Fred Shapiro, National Security Advisor, blurted out in surprise, "Are you suggesting we do nothing about this?"

"Certainly not, but aren't we here to make decisions that take us toward our ultimate goal of peace? The question becomes one of deciding if peace really can be achieved through force. We have thousands of years of history that indicate violence doesn't work to achieve peace in the long run."

White House Chief of Staff, Mike Simons, had never heard his friend and boss speak this way in their many years together. He asked the obvious question, "What are you proposing we should do?"

Matt appreciated that Mike had provided the perfect lead-in to introduce his new strategy. "We've all been spinning our wheels trying to figure out how to put the toothpaste back in the tube. I believe that conflicts between nations won't be healed by using violence to achieve peace. What we need to do is establish our mutual points of agreement and build on those to achieve greater and sustainable solutions that will work to the good of all."

The silence in the room was as profound as the implied challenge the President had just placed before them. Matt could feel the questions swimming around in the room, albeit unspoken. Questions like, "What points of agreement?" "Don't the Muslim nations largely believe that all infidels are abominations before Allah?" "What about the families of our soldiers who have died over there? Don't they deserve to see justice done to those who murdered their sons and daughters?" "The Muslim nations don't trust us. They don't respect us. They believe America is nothing more than a spoiled child who has not been around long enough to understand how the world works. In perhaps a thousand years the Americans will mature, but they have a long way to go before they have the right to sit at the table with their elders."

Matt reflected on what he believed was the real conflict. He decided this was the time to start being completely transparent and lay all his cards on the table. "Let's forget about the past for a moment. We all know the real issue is the long-term economic survival of the Middle East nations." He paused to look around the room. Matt was thankful to see they were still listening with interest. Feeling optimistic, he continued. "These countries currently rely on crude oil to supply as much as ninety percent of their revenues from exports. Since those desert nations have little else to sell to the rest of the world, the clock is ticking when it comes to establishing their permanent place in the global economy.

"If the Middle East nations don't manage to shift into sustainable products and services in say the next fifty years, the world's need for energy will be forced to look elsewhere to protect their own long-term interests. If we want to find lasting solutions to the conflicts in that region, offering them hope for a prosperous economic future is a great start. Giving them reason to trust in our good intentions is crucial. Figuring out how to get all nations to recognize that each person in the world is a valued member of our shared family is the key."

The entire NSC was stunned. They all wondered what had happened to their President since his heart attack. His proposal was the kind of talk that sounded good after many drinks with a close friend, but this meeting was about hard reality. These terrorists played for keeps as well as by different fundamental rules. Many of the NSC members feared that if Matt actually went down this road that it would further disrupt the ongoing Middle East conflicts as well as the continuous flow of oil to the U.S.

President Alexander could see they all needed to take a break to think about what he had said. He told the NSC members that each person would be polled for their best suggestions when they reconvened in a few hours.

★★★

George Salazar was a teenager when he was told that his father, Major George Salazar Sr., had been captured in Vietnam. The whole family was counting on a prisoner exchange to see the patriarch of the Salazar household returned home. The Paris Peace Accord did arrange the release of all remaining American soldiers, but George's father was not among them. The Vietnamese government records briefly stated that "he died in captivity."

When George became an adult, he had already chosen his career. He wanted to join the CIA. He never spoke of his real motivation for this, but the family knew he was still looking for his father. He hoped that working for the CIA would give him the access and contacts he needed to find and bring his dad home.

It turned out that George had a real talent for his job. He was an excellent agent who always managed to complete his missions. When he became a team leader, his successes continued and so did the promotions. He became known for his creative solutions to tricky problems and his excellent record gained him a lot of leeway to complete his missions.

George was quickly promoted to a level where he could investigate his father's "missing in action" status in Vietnam. He discovered that sketchy records of his father's imprisonment existed from the first months of his capture. Years had passed without further status reports in any of the CIA's files. George became convinced that his father might still be alive and let his superiors know what he'd discovered.

Despite his pleas for help, no one wanted to open up that can of worms with the Vietnamese government. George pushed the matter until he was called on the carpet and told he'd have to let the matter go or face disciplinary action. Outwardly, he heeded the advice and no longer mentioned his father to anyone. Inwardly, he vowed to rise high enough in the CIA's ranks to discover the truth and rescue his father if he was still alive.

Years later, when he became the head of the CIA, George finally learned it had not ended well for his father. Unofficially, he contacted people outside of normal channels who knew of his father's imprisonment. Their information was that Salazar Sr. remained captive in Vietnam even after the Paris Peace Accord had arranged for the release of all American prisoners. George's father had been so brutally tortured by his captors that releasing him to be displayed to the international media was not an option. He died, still in prison, a few years after he should have returned home.

George knew there was nothing he could have done personally to rescue his father, but there were many in the United States government who could have saved him. An intense resentment filled George that was focused on the Washington bureaucrats who were too timid to do the right thing. It wasn't just his father's welfare, but the entire country that had been damaged by our government's lack of action in Vietnam. George swore he would never put politics or his own career ahead of the welfare of the country.

★★★

Dr. Jerome Westcott was in charge of digital forensics at CIA headquarters in Langley, Virginia. The damaged laptop computer had been brought directly to him from the site of the underground bunker in Israel. He was assured that before the battery ran down, this old beat up laptop had been functional. Not only was it several years old, but the power supply and battery configuration had been modified from the manufacturer's original design. The challenge now was to make sure he connected the right voltage and amps to power it back up without frying any of the components. He heard that agents had died getting this laptop from the terrorists. Failure to download the data stored on its hard drive was not an option.

Jerome removed the battery from the laptop and applied a low voltage trickle charge to revive it. Over several hours, he increased the voltage slightly until the indicator showed it was fully charged. He took the necessary readings and set his lab's power supply to match the battery's optimum output. He then fired up the laptop with a new hard drive that was compatible with the existing motherboard. He was not misinformed. This unit was fully functional when it had enough juice.

Next came the most important step. Dr. Westcott made a cloned image of the laptop's hard drive. The original drive would contain traces of deleted files that were not recoverable from a copied drive. If he could get the cloned drive to boot up without something going wrong, he would then try it with the original hard drive.

He clicked the icon telling his test computer to boot off the copied drive. After a few moments, the operating system logo appeared. Then the drive started to execute a command that was hidden deep within the boot sector. It was programmed to reformat itself to remove all files or traces of files it might contain if it was ever rebooted.

Dr. Westcott quickly cut the power and the monitor went black. It was a good thing he took this precaution or he might have lost everything. The bad news was that this project would take far longer than he originally estimated to salvage the recoverable data off the hard drive. He would have to dissect the boot up sequence's machine code to safely locate the self-destruct program hidden within. He did not look forward to reporting this delay to the Director. Jerome thought Salazar had been in a really foul mood lately.

Chapter 7

Matt needed some time to reflect and rest up for their next NSC meeting and the Oval Office was not the best place to relax. Instead, he walked through to the White House residence. He settled on the couch in the family room trying to make sense of his own thoughts. He was asleep where he sat when Erin walked in a few minutes later. She took a seat at the other end of the couch, careful not to wake him. The stress of recent events was also taking its toll on Erin. She too had trouble focusing her thoughts as she drifted off to sleep.

★★★

Matt realized he was back in the nondescript room again. The other man looked like Amelius at first glance, including the glow around his body, but there were subtle differences. The next moment Erin was at Matt's side looking bewildered at having arrived so abruptly.

"What? Wait...what the heck is this?" she said looking around in all directions.

"Welcome! My name is Ariel. You don't remember me quite yet but we have worked together before."

Matt was quicker to find his bearings and asked, "Where is Amelius?"

Erin looked at Matt and stammered, "You know what's going on here? Who is Amelius and who are you?" she said pointing toward Ariel.

"There is nothing here that threatens you," said Ariel. "Our work together in the past was the same as it is now; repairing your relationship. You were once the perfect couple as both soulmates and the best of friends.

Now you don't trust each other, you don't respect each other and you rarely agree on anything."

"Amelius said something about you the last time I was here. So you're a marriage counselor or something?" Matt asked.

"The 'or something' is closer to the truth, but I accept the role of counselor as things stand between you now," Ariel answered.

Erin was clearly bewildered and frustrated. "Am I the only one who doesn't know what's going on here?"

Ariel smiled, "You will soon remember our previous encounters. Relax and allow your subconscious mind to acclimate as it takes control. While you are in physical form, that is to say, when you are awake, the subconscious mind is often blocked out by the conscious mind."

Matt groaned, "I'm remembering all right. Every time we've met like this in the past, things only became worse back on earth."

Erin too was beginning to remember. Ariel had been trying to help them work through the conflicts in their relationship. At the end of those sessions, her heart would become light with hope. Then they would wake up and go back to 'business as usual.' In fact, tensions were often worse because they became even more frustrated with each other. "And so here we are again. Why should we expect anything to improve given our history with these sessions?"

That's an excellent question!" Ariel went on to explain, "The challenges in your relationship are temporary and not without purpose. Matt chose to go down a different path in order to become the President. You stayed the course you were on and that disagreement caused most of your conflicts. Neither of you was right nor wrong in this. But now you can, and should, come together despite the suffering each has caused the other. You truly are soul mates and it is time to heal this earthly rift in your relationship."

"All our talks turn into fights. What makes you think we can heal our marriage now when things have only become worse over time?" Erin said with frustration.

Ariel answered patiently, "In the same way that people often wait until just before a deadline to accomplish an important task, you two have arrived at that point. Matt's heart attack, the conflicts in the Holy Land, the lack of agreement among members of the NSC, and the challenges in your marriage have all converged to bring this unique opportunity to fruition. If you do not heal your relationship at this juncture, you won't be able to successfully navigate that which is about to unfold in your lives. The well-being and happiness of literally billions of people are riding on your decision."

As Ariel's words echoed in their minds, their vision was filled with scenario after scenario of the choices they might make in the near future. None of them were easy and all of them were frightening, even those with the best outcomes imaginable. There was a real chance that another world war would be the result if they diverged from a very narrow path of choices. Perhaps the scariest part was having so much responsibility for seeing the plan through this critical period. They had to remember how to love and trust each other again as they had in the early years of their relationship. They had seen the potential of a better life play out into the future and agreed this was what they both wanted, but the harsh truth of the 'real world' conspired to push them apart each day of their waking lives.

Matt asked skeptically, "What can we do differently this time so that we heal these old wounds and become best friends again?"

"That is a hopeful step forward for it is the first time you've thought to ask me that question," beamed Ariel. "Your subconscious mind is in control right now and it is ideally the guide of your conscious mind on earth. Like an architect, we are here drafting the plans for your earthly lives and relationship. But a design is only as good as the actual contractor who puts the structure together."

Erin cut in, frustrated, "Didn't you say that the subconscious mind is usually blocked by the conscious mind when we're awake? How can the subconscious be our guide if our conscious mind never lets it be heard?"

"You make an excellent point," soothed Ariel. "It takes practice to listen to our inner voice, our conscience, but like exercising a muscle, the more you make use of it, the stronger it grows. You have been working on this for years and it is now time to put your love and trust into action. You must believe that you are ready if this is to succeed."

Matt was clearly distraught as he responded, "Even the best scenarios and choices you showed us place Erin in real danger, in some cases to the point of her being killed! How can I possibly respond patiently and peacefully when she is in great danger?"

"Matt, you are unique in that you are humankind's best chance at walking the narrow path you see before you. You are correct that Erin faces the possibility of great danger, but if you don't succeed and she does die in the effort, it would be a blessing. If you fail, no one will want to be on earth for the horrific violence that follows. You know you do not desire to start a world war no matter what happens, so focus on that and you will be constantly guided to persevere in this laudable quest. Erin volunteered for this solemn mission long ago and she may yet survive to help you achieve a lasting peace," Ariel said with conviction.

Erin started to ask another question, but the room began to fade as someone nudged her shoulder.

★★★

Matt woke to find Erin sleeping next to him on the couch. He shook her gently. She sat up and rubbed her eyes as he moved toward the door.

Erin said, "You don't have to leave. In fact, I came here to talk with you."

He started to cut her off with a typical sarcastic response. Something made him stop from saying out loud, "The last thing I need right now is another of your one-way conversations where 'we' explore my short-comings." Matt reconsidered what to say. If he was honest with himself, he knew deep within that it wasn't all her fault that they had grown apart. He rarely responded to her observations; and that meant that her unintended monologues were as much his fault as they were hers. He laughed ruefully to himself when he admitted the truth. He remembered thinking it would be easier to negotiate a lasting peace in the Middle East than to restore the loving relationship he once had with his wife. Then something flashed through his mind. He didn't understand why, but somehow he knew that avoiding this talk would have dire consequences.

"What did you want to talk about?" he asked cautiously, softening his tone.

"I hear you made quite a statement in the NSC meeting this morning." Matt just nodded. Erin continued, "Are you really considering a change in Middle East policy and strategy at this crucial point?"

"It seemed appropriate to me," he replied. "Nothing else was working."

"Would you be revealing state secrets by telling me what you have in mind?" she asked.

Matt laughed. "Actually, my new strategy for resolving the challenges in the Middle East is to do away with state secrets." He described his proposal to the NSC members to help wean those countries away from their dependence on oil exports. He outlined his vision for all nations to achieve such peaceful prosperity by truly trusting each other. This could be accomplished by pursuing only win/win scenarios for all concerned on each issue. Trust would be built by all nations living up to their agreements and accepting all people as equal members of the same family.

Surprised, Erin had no quick response for him. She too was wondering about Matt's change of heart, so she finally asked, "What happened since your heart attack to change your mind like this?"

Matt winced hearing the question that no member of the NSC had dared to voice. He hesitated to discuss it knowing her deep disappointment with him simmered on so many levels. Still, if he couldn't be honest about this with Erin, who else could he trust to help him see this through? If transparency was truly the answer, he had to trust that his vision for a peaceful world could start with the woman he had married.

He tried again to fully recall his extraordinary experience after his collapse. He started to describe the unusual briefing with the man in glowing white when a tremendous feeling of déjà vu washed over him. He had already experienced this same conversation with Erin. It was playing again like a familiar movie. The man in the odd room had shown this particular scene to Matt to encourage him to persevere in accomplishing a difficult task. Matt understood that the choices he and Erin were about to make would affect many events that had yet to unfold.

He did his best to explain what he was thinking and feeling as well as what his conscience was guiding him to do. Erin listened intently but gave nothing away in her body language or expression. Matt finally had to ask if she thought he was going crazy.

Her reply surprised him. "Honestly, this is the first time you've sounded like a sane person in years. I don't know what to think of your briefing room experience or what that man showed you, but I do think that you just offered a logical approach to resolving the Middle East conflicts. I'm not saying it will succeed. It probably won't when you look at every event and attitude that would have to align in the world for your plan to work. That doesn't change the fact that starting over fresh and helping everyone to succeed is the best way to achieve world peace."

Matt felt his eyes moisten as he realized she was with him instead of against him on this. How many years had he felt that Erin just didn't understand what it took to succeed in politics? For how long had he been shying away from deep conversations with her because she no longer saw things as he did? It felt good to be on the same page as his wife. He had forgotten that her moral compass was usually spot-on accurate.

★★★

When the President returned to the Situation Room, everyone stood but there was no round of applause this time. He could tell by their expressions that this was going to be a tough meeting. If he read the room correctly, their concern wasn't necessarily that they disagreed with his suggestion. Like Erin said, the plan could work in theory, but all odds were against it. They took their seats and waited for Matt to begin.

"A lot has happened today. We uncovered vital intel on the terrorists. We opened discussions that could change our entire strategy and policies for the Middle East. I know this has been quite a reversal from where we started just over a week ago and that's why I want to hear from each of the NSC Directors and Statuary Attendees. I want to hear your thoughts on how you think we should proceed. Let's start with Eric."

The Vice President cleared his throat, sighed and quietly began. "Mr. President, the concept of starting over by establishing our mutual points of agreement and developing fresh ideas with an emphasis on trust is a good one. We have think-tanks that recommend such an approach all the time and not just for resolving conflicts in the Middle East. The reason those recommendations have never been implemented is because they won't work unless everyone agrees to play by the same rules. In my opinion, the majority of the people living in the Middle East, including the moderates, see no reason to 'play nice' with infidels.

"I believe that your ideas have merit and should be explored further in hopes that they might work someday. However, in light of all I just said, I do not feel the Middle East is a good place, nor is this a good time, to test a new strategy for achieving peace."

Secretary of State Joan Hartley spoke next. "The Vice President has articulated much of my thinking as well. I might add that I'm not sure what 'points of agreement' we could build upon with terrorists who believe non-Muslims are an abomination before Allah. Setting religious beliefs aside, few countries would define world peace in the same way let alone agree on how we might get there."

Secretary of Defense Steve Lombard added his opinion. "Mr. President, it will be almost impossible to get terrorists to trust that we are being completely honest and have no hidden agenda to take advantage of them with this new approach. I believe they would only agree to your proposal if they thought doing so would relax our guard. The Vice President was correct when he implied that the U.S. has become the ultimate infidel to many of the Muslim people. If they believe that making peace with us is tantamount to making peace with the devil, can we really expect them to deal with us honorably?"

General McComb continued on the theme. "I have to agree there. It's not just trying to get the people of the Middle East to trust us; it's trying to get all of us to trust them in return. I know I'm not going to have faith in any agreements we make with Middle Eastern leaders until a long list of grievances have been addressed first."

Director of National Intelligence Lieutenant General Richard Newman spoke next. "I find I can't remain unbiased in this either, sir. My days are spent finding and stopping people who would take great pleasure in killing off every single American and believe they are doing Allah's will in the process. Just because we decide that the violence has gone on long enough does not mean everyone else will agree. Secretary Hartley made a great point that few nations will define world peace in the same way.

Even if we could agree on a definition, the chances of everyone agreeing on a process for achieving global peace would be slim at best."

Director of the CIA George Salazar added, "Like Director Newman, I work to frustrate the plans and efforts of terrorists on a daily basis. At any moment there are literally thousands of people thinking of how they might kill us. Getting people with that mindset to think seriously about achieving a true and lasting peace is a wasted effort. They are far too committed to vengeance and justice through killing off their enemies for me to believe they will change their ways now."

Gil Kowalski, Director of National Drug Control Policy, was last to speak. "I regret I was unable to attend the meeting last week because I was in the Yucatan peninsula with a dozen of my South and Central American counterparts. It sounds like I missed a lot." Everyone laughed lightly at his understatement. "Like so many others here, my responsibilities keep me in constant touch with some of the worst criminals in the world. One thing I will say about most of the drug lords, they make decisions according to their own best interests. In my experience, the President's proposed strategy has a slim chance to succeed. We have to convince everyone involved that this peace initiative will make them richer and happier without putting them in greater danger. Figure out the points of agreement that lead to that goal and you just might be on your way to a viable new strategy."

The room fell silent again as they waited to see how the President would respond to the overwhelming lack of support for his proposal. Matt too was silent but his mind was racing. He was not surprised by their skepticism, in fact, he had agreed with them just days before. He needed to show that a peaceful response did not ignore all their opinions and sage advice. He knew from experience that he needed to adequately address all their concerns. Once there were no more objections, the only alternative left would be to support his proposal. Just as the silence was becoming uncomfortable, he was suddenly inspired.

"Actually," Matt began, "I'm glad to see that we have so much agreement already on such a controversial topic. My own thoughts on the main issues, namely trust and seeing the enemy as part of our larger family, were echoed in most of the opinions expressed around this table. I was especially interested in Gil's comments because I think he offered the key to everyone's objections. The new approach I'm talking about must begin with convincing everyone they will ultimately be better off helping my proposal to succeed."

"Can you give us a specific example, Mr. President?" said Eric Jefferson, who was a bit surprised Matt was still pursuing this line of thinking.

"Of course. In fact, let's start with our own challenges between conservatives and liberals. Let's say that a new bill is brought before Congress that would provide better food, housing and medical care for underprivileged children. We can all guess where the lines would be drawn in debating this issue. The conservatives would be against it and the liberals for it. Each side would end up thinking the other is wrong, either for wasting money and raising taxes or for being stingy and having no compassion for those in need. The usual negotiations to get such a bill passed would bring out the worst in all of us. We would become polarized in our positions and attempt to massage the bill until it doesn't really accomplish anything. The inevitable bad feelings make it tougher for opposing sides to trust each other with every new debate. It's easy to see that we already have tough challenges at home, albeit without the violence, when compared to the Middle East."

The leaders around the table mumbled their mixed reactions to the President's example. Where he was going with this was still anyone's guess.

Matt continued, "I think it's safe to say that it would be impossible to get 100 percent agreement on the bill in question using the same arguments and process we always have. But, what if we approached this differently? What if we invited all of Congress to a meeting where we lined up ten homeless children who would be helped by the proposed legislation? What if we took a vote among the 500-plus elected officials asking which of those kids should be denied better shelter, food and health care? Do we think anyone would deny them such help on principle? Since we still have underprivileged children, it becomes clear that our system is flawed in accomplishing that laudable goal. That is what I mean by starting out fresh by finding our points of agreement."

They nodded their general accord, at least in the example he provided. Who would want America's homeless children to go without food, shelter or proper medical care? Still, finding just one point they could agree upon would not resolve all the other underlying issues involved in making that happen.

Matt was encouraged by the change he could see in their faces. "The real conflict is not whether or not we should all help these kids to have a better life; it is in how we can best accomplish that goal. Once we are clear everyone is willing to help, we can move on to asking better questions such as; 'Who is best equipped to make it happen?' 'How do we fund this effort?' 'If we could start fresh, what solutions would make this a win/win for everyone concerned?'"

Joan Hartley interjected, "Mr. President, this is an interesting exercise on paper, but in the real world your approach is unrealistic. We can't simply undo overnight the long standing political processes that have made us who we are today. Cumbersome as it may be, working within the system is still the best way to go about organizing all the power and money it takes to help the children you mentioned."

Matt recognized that Jane's slight shift in the topic indicated he was making progress. "Perhaps, but let's go back to our situation in the Middle East. Suppose tomorrow everyone on the earth unilaterally agreed to stop all violence for twenty four hours? And then what if we all agreed to extend the peace for a second day, then a third and so on? Hypothetically, this could happen tomorrow without passing any legislation. In many ways, our 'long-standing system' of doing things the way they've always been done is an addiction we must overcome. We continually stand in our own way to avoid change instead of achieving our most important goals. Much like alcoholics in a twelve-step program need to decide for themselves not to drink for just one more day, the world could change its violent ways immediately if each individual agrees to try."

Matt pointed to Director Kowalski noticing he had a point to make. "My job in the war against drugs helps me to understand a lot about addictive behavior. Addicts fall off the wagon all the time, even when they are in rehab. How many 'violence addicts' worldwide does it take to fall off the wagon before things return to what I hesitate to call normal?"

"That's a valid question," Matt said, "but see how quickly it takes us back to familiar old fears and patterns. Perhaps a better way to phrase the question would be, 'When so many people support righteous retribution against their enemies, how does a peace initiative ever get started?' Clearly one side has to go first and not second-guess themselves while setting a peaceful example."

General McComb argued, "That approach won't work. The Muslims will never stop using violence against us unless it's out of fear of our reprisals. Don't forget that to them we are infidels and deserve whatever damage and suffering they can inflict upon us."

National Security Advisor Fred Shapiro interjected, "I feel compelled to add my two cents here considering that I have deep family roots in the region. General McComb has said that achieving a peaceful coexistence between Muslims and infidels won't work. I recall that in 1947 India and Pakistan became free sovereign nations largely through civil disobedience aimed at Great Britain. The Hindus and Muslims fought fiercely among themselves, but the gentle leadership of Mohandas Gandhi had a remarkable effect on all sides of those conflicts. My point is that President Alexander's peace initiative has a precedent that eventually worked between the British, Hindus and Muslims."

Matt took back the floor at this point saying, "Thank you for that reminder, Fred. Perhaps we don't have to reinvent the wheel here. We can scrutinize what Gandhi did right less than 100 years ago. It wasn't perfect but it was far better than an all-out war to resolve their differences. Asking ourselves, 'What can we do today to improve on his success?' is a great example of framing better questions.

"Actually, I'm going to leave all this as 'questions to ponder' for the moment. I want everyone to consider what has been shared for our next meeting. I find this subject fascinating, but there is a lot more to running this country than pursuing peace in the Middle East. I'm late for several meetings on domestic issues. We'll pick this up tomorrow."

Chapter 8

General McComb, Lieutenant General Newman and Director Salazar shared a limousine ride to their next meeting. That would be a briefing on developments from the evidence discovered in and around the underground bunker in Israel. The four-star General set the tone for the discussion. "Have you ever heard a bigger load of crap in your life? Alexander thinks the peaceful resistance trick Gandhi pulled in India will actually work again in the Middle East. Does he really believe we can ever trust a terrorist?"

George Salazar added, "I was thinking the same thing, but he is apparently convinced his plan will work."

Rick Newman's agreement made it unanimous, "It does seem to be a recipe for disaster with no upside for the U.S. I wonder what 'come to Jesus meeting' happened after his heart attack to make the President change his mind? It seems like he's done a one-eighty on us."

McComb said, "I don't care if God Himself came down to set him straight. Trying to achieve peace through trust and nonviolence is a temporary fix at best and just damn unrealistic. I'm guessing it will take a lot more murder and mayhem before he comes to his senses and changes his mind again. It felt like we were so close to doing the right thing just a few days ago but now we're back to square one."

"So what are we going to do about this?" Newman asked.

Salazar replied, "We know it's just a matter of time before the President sees the error of his ways. His peace initiative won't succeed no matter what we do. But I think the passive approach he prefers can actually be used to help speed things along. I believe he will quickly discover the wisdom behind aggressively ending all Middle Eastern conflicts."

McComb and Newman had the same question, "What did you have in mind?"

"In the CIA, we specialize in circumventing terrorist plots before they become reality. We often arrest or otherwise remove the key people before they can carry out an attack. What if, in the spirit of cooperative nonviolence, we just sit back and watch for a while? Even if a vast majority of the countries agree to a policy of nonviolence, there will always be someone who sees this as the perfect time to make themselves heard. The idea is to rectify the President's good, albeit misguided, intentions before he goes too far. I want to nip this in the bud before he announces this plan publicly and tries to sell it to the world."

McComb and Newman pondered this. The approach had merit. After all, Salazar's suggestion was in keeping with the nonviolent intent of the President's proposal and it could make the point quickly. They also knew that it would be Salazar and his people who would catch the heat if things backfired. They couldn't see any downside to the plan.

"I like it," said McComb. "How long before we might see some tangible results?"

"It would probably become noticeable within a few weeks. And understand that I will continue to stop any activity that might interfere with the greater good of the United States."

Newman asked, "Don't you think others might become suspicious once you lower the level of surveillance on these groups?"

Salazar smiled in response. "Not really. I just have to keep rotating my people to cover different activities. I can leave unnoticed holes in our surveillance for short periods so that certain groups will be temporarily off our radar. Their violent acts will seem to occur despite our efforts to stop them instead of passively allowing some tragic events to run their course."

All three men considered the implications. Salazar's plan would serve to show the President the error of his ways by not interfering with the militant factions of the Middle East. They each sincerely felt this was a bold but necessary step that had to be taken for the good of the United States. They rode the rest of the way in silence as their car passed well-known Washington landmarks, each lost in his own thoughts.

★★★

Riding quietly in the limousine, McComb found himself remembering one of the worst days of his life. He did this frequently enough that it bordered on obsession. That day had proved to define him and his bias against a peaceful approach toward the radicals of the Middle East. Until that day, he had believed in peace through strength and that the role of the military was one of deterrence rather than aggression.

He had won many honors on the battlefield as a young officer in Vietnam, a Silver Star with Valor among them. When his son Martin Jr. said that he too wanted to follow his father's path into the Army, General McComb supported him all the way. He wished now that he could take it back.

Martin Jr. had quickly risen to the rank of Major and specialized in G2 intelligence at the battalion level. His 3rd Battalion, 187th Infantry Regiment, also known as the Iron Rakkasans, was scheduled to pull out of Iraq in a few months. So in August, Major Martin McComb, Jr. was part of the team training the newly organized Iraqi troops to take over all counterinsurgency efforts in the coming months. He oversaw the "checkpoint training" near Yusufiyah to keep terrorists and their murderous ordinance from getting inside the larger cities.

Just before noon on that terrible day, a bus rolled up behind the queue of vehicles approaching the checkpoint. The old school bus was painted an ugly off white with flat house paint. 'Saint Boniface Catholic School' was crudely stenciled in black block letters on the sides to identify the alma mater of the young teenagers inside. There were very few non-Muslim schools in Iraq so this bus caught everyone's attention. Major McComb became interested and walked over to investigate.

A soldier instructed the driver to step out of the bus while telling the teenagers to remain seated. Once the driver was outside, the other soldiers went about the task of inspecting the vehicle for any explosives or passengers who didn't belong. Major McComb was curious enough to question the driver directly about the school. Mustafa didn't speak English but did his best to answer McComb's questions through an interpreter.

Apparently he had only worked for the school a short time. He admitted that it was "just a job" and laughed politely when asked if he was Catholic. The school specialized in educating teens who were orphaned by the war and it was funded by several Catholic churches in the United States. When asked where the priests or nuns were, Mustafa indicated their car had broken down in the last town but he expected them to catch up soon at this checkpoint. He then asked if they could wait for their arrival as long as he parked the bus out of the flow of traffic. The soldiers had finished their inspection so Major McComb allowed Mustafa to pull the bus over to the side to wait for the priests to arrive.

The teenagers poured out of the hot bus and stood in the meager shade it created. The light breeze and fresh air made standing outside preferable to remaining seated. Major McComb kept an eye on the continuing vehicle inspections while he asked more questions of Mustafa. Martin Jr. was fascinated with this country and wondered what life was really like for an Iraqi national who lived in this war-torn land of violence. Mustafa seemed unconcerned with religion or politics while doing his best to earn a living wherever there was work to be had.

A few soldiers who were not currently inspecting vehicles also gathered around to listen and enjoy the break from their routine. There may have been as many as forty men and boys crowded together in the stingy shade of the bus. Mustafa said via the translator that he didn't believe life in Iraq would always be full of security checkpoints and violence. He told them he was certain that peace would eventually come to his country because that was Allah's will. When McComb asked him how he thought there could ever be peace here after thousands of years of violence, Mustafa took that as the sign he'd been waiting for.

★★★

In his mind, Mustafa flashed back to the events of that same morning. He managed to punch a small hole in the oil line of the priests' car without anyone seeing him. By his calculations, it would break down before reaching their destination, the history museum in Yusufiyah. As they were passing a small town, the car's engine froze up from the lack of oil. Convincing the priests to let Mustafa proceed and wait for them at the main checkpoint while they acquired another car was the key to his plan. He would have a good reason to wait by the checkpoint if none of the clergymen were with him.

Two of the priests had volunteered to ride on the bus, but Mustafa assured them there was no need. An air-conditioned car could easily catch up to the aging bus and it was surprisingly hot that day. The teenagers were used to the climate so it was not such a hardship on them. The priests relented with a promise from Mustafa that he would wait for them at the checkpoint and return if they didn't show up within an hour or two.

He couldn't believe how well his plan was unfolding. The American and Iraqi soldiers did not seem suspicious of him and they even became friendly. Their rapid questions seemed to be out of genuine curiosity rather than an interrogation of one whom they did not trust. When more of the soldiers edged closer to hear his description of life in the villages of Iraq, Mustafa prayed for a sign that he was indeed doing Allah's will.

Suddenly, the priests' car pulled to a stop behind the school bus and they walked over to join the crowd. The American Major had just asked Mustafa a question that told him the time had come. The Major wanted to know how a lasting peace could ever come to Iraq. Mustafa had been taught since he was young that infidels, people who did not believe Allah was the one true God and Mohammed was His prophet, were the reason why there could be no peace. Once everyone believed in the loving ways of Allah, peace would be the natural result. However, the infidels must be eliminated in order to attain peace on earth.

Mustafa decided this was the perfect time to detonate the C-4 explosive vest he had concealed under his loose shirt. If he could wipe out forty or fifty of the infidels while serving the will of Allah in such a holy way, he was assured of attaining heaven.

He looked around at the group and then directly at Major McComb. He said in Arabic, "All you need to know to achieve peace in Iraq and throughout the world is Allahu Akbar!" Before the interpreter could translate "God is the greatest," Mustafa pulled the detonator pin and his vest exploded. The blast killed thirty-two people, including himself and Major McComb, while injuring twenty one other men and boys.

★★★

General McComb shook his head to end his morbid reverie. He took a deep breath and released it slowly to clear his mind before exiting the limousine with Newman and Salazar. He had pieced together the story of his son's murder from the survivors of the attack at the checkpoint to Yusufiyah. The soldiers had treated the terrorist with polite kindness and a sincere desire to understand life from his perspective. They dropped their guard because they trusted that the bus driver's intentions were simply to help the orphaned teenagers as he earned a living for himself.

How could anyone who felt the pain of cruel attacks like this ever believe there could be trust between enemies, let alone a lasting peace in the Middle East? Martin McComb had lost his son learning that hard lesson. He would be damned if he'd let his fellow Americans suffer as he had if he could stop it. Surely the only way to achieve true peace in the Middle East was to eliminate the terrorists and anyone who supported them. If these animals could be captured, tried in a court of law and jailed, that would be acceptable to him. If they died resisting, McComb would not lose any sleep over their deaths. Killing terrorists was simple justice for having caused the deaths of so many innocent people, including his son.

Chapter 9

Matt was in the White House residence living room. With him were Vice President Eric Jefferson, Secretary of State Joan Hartley and Secretary of Defense Steve Lombard. He had called them together informally to answer their questions offline and let them know what he planned to do next.

"Eric," he began, "why don't you start us off? Ask me anything that's on your mind with regard to the situation in the Holy Land."

"Mr. President, you seem to have made a complete reversal of the position you took just prior to your medical scare. You started out saying WMDs were on the table. Now it seems a peaceful response is your intention. Where are we really headed?"

"That seems to be the question on everyone's mind," Matt observed. "The truth is that life-threatening experience caused me to review my goals and priorities, not just personally, but from a strategic and tactical perspective for the country. Being the leader of the world's most powerful army does not help me look for peaceful solutions when we're provoked... quite the opposite in fact. My time off after the heart attack helped me remember an old saying: Just because we have the ability to beat up every other country in the world doesn't mean we should.

"Years ago, when I was first elected to Congress, I worked hard to win the hearts and minds of my constituents and even my enemies. I realize now how lazy I became thinking I didn't have to win over anyone as long as I could overpower them into submission. That was a mistake and I deeply regret it. The good news is that I've found myself again and now resolve to keep my eye on the ball."

Joan said, "Saying our response might include WMDs put the taste of blood in the mouths of some very powerful people on the NSC. How do you propose to gain their cooperation after the events in Israel got their blood boiling in the first place?"

"The truth is I can't do much about that. I can admit I was headed in a direction that needed to change. I can also meet with them privately, as we are doing now, to see if we can come to an agreement that will give my nonviolent policies a chance."

Steve frowned, "And what will you do if they don't come around?"

"I'm not against firing anyone for insubordination," Matt replied, "but they are all good people who deserve to be a part of this historic effort to change the world. If they choose to oppose my peace plan, I'll have to deal with that as it comes."

Eric asked, "So what is our next step? Do we just ignore the biological attacks and the destruction of the compound in Israel? That was the most aggressive threat against our people since 9/11."

Matt paused for a moment and chose his words carefully. "There is a huge difference between doing nothing and using only amicable means to accomplish a goal. I am prepared to personally meet with the leaders of the Middle Eastern nations to present my vision for a peaceful world. And I intend to do this immediately. I still want our investigators to positively identify the guilty parties involved in these attacks. However, my future plans will focus on encouraging and inspiring those who distrust and hate us more than establishing blame."

Joan was shocked, "You mean you're going to ask the Muslim leaders to come to the U.S. to meet with you with little or no notice? Most of them will appreciate the chance to publicly decline your invitation using the media to do so."

Matt made it clear he was serious. "I will not ask them to come here. I plan to go to the Middle East, unannounced, and meet with each of them on their turf. I am resolute when I say that 'full disclosure' is our best chance to win their respect, trust and cooperation. The usual political positioning games must be set aside to give peace a proper chance to work."

Now Steve expressed surprise. "Go there unannounced? Word is bound to get out and make you an easy target for perhaps a million angry people who would love to see you dead. Are you sure this is a good idea?"

"Absolutely! I will keep my itinerary secret and strictly need-to-know regarding how long we'll be there, how we'll be traveling, and where we'll be staying. If Osama Bin Laden can hide from us for more than a decade, I'm sure we can figure out how to keep me out of harm's way for a few days even with Armageddon nearby. I am willing to use whatever means necessary to stay off everyone's radar while I am in the region, including disguising myself and using my doubles. My sincerity and faith in this plan cannot be conveyed properly unless I am face-to-face with the people I am asking to trust us."

Joan, realizing that she would be at the President's side for the duration of this risky plan, asked, "Just how do you expect the heads of state of all those countries to react when you show up on their doorsteps without warning?"

"The 'unannounced' part is intended to serve many purposes," Matt replied. "First, we issue a press release that says our Secretary of State is going overseas to meet with her Middle Eastern counterparts while I am resting at Camp David. The press will not expect to see me for a few days so the cover story is plausible enough. Joan, you will work quickly to set these appointments and I will accompany you, in disguise, to each one. When we are behind closed doors with as few witnesses as we can manage, I'll reveal my presence and ask to speak alone with the head of each country in turn. I intend to personally present my vision for the future and how we will get there together without fanfare or media coverage."

Eric quipped, "I may want to be President someday but I don't want to get there like this. It seems suicidal to expose yourself in this way, especially under such precarious circumstances. This may sound indelicate, but just what will we do if they manage to assassinate you on this trip?"

"The Office of the President," Matt stated, "is not just a person, it's an ongoing position. You need to be ready to take over in case the worst happens. I am confident that you will do a great job if anything does happen to me, but I have no plans of dying on this trip. If I wasn't positive that this will work, I wouldn't take such a risk.

"Eric and Joan, I need you both to arrange the private meetings and prepare an announcement for the media. Steve, I'll need you to help me explain this to Generals McComb and Newman as well as to George Salazar. You have a better relationship with them, especially in light of my new strategy."

"I'll set that up for tomorrow morning," Steve assured Matt.

"But first," Matt sighed, "I have to explain it to Erin."

★★★

When they said their good nights and left him alone, Matt walked over to the door that led to the master bedroom. Erin was still awake and reading a book as he entered.

"How did today go?" she asked.

"About as well as it could, I suppose." Matt exhaled loudly and sat down next to her on the side of the bed. "I need to bring you up to speed on a few things that are coming up."

He described his idea to secretly travel to the Middle East while telling the media they were going to Camp David for a few days. Matt was doing his best to reassure Erin that he was in little danger if they followed his plan to keep his trip quiet until he returned. She didn't say a word the entire time. When he finally finished, he gave her his best presidential smile as his way of giving her the floor.

"And you want me to stay at Camp David keeping the reporters occupied until you return?" she asked.

"I wouldn't have put it quite like that, but essentially yes," Matt replied sheepishly.

"I have a better idea. I think I should go with you on this trip. I know I'm not part of the political meetings, but I want to be with you the rest of the time. You said yourself that it should be safe and I support whole-heartedly what you are trying to do. You will need all the moral support you can get and someone has to keep an eye on you in case you have any more health problems. You say you have no plans to die over there...well prove it by taking me with you for all those reasons and more. Hey, it's the Middle East. Women are barely noticed. I'll keep myself respectfully covered up and no one will ever know I was there."

Matt didn't have much room to argue with her. He rarely did. He had always admired her wisdom, judgment and quick mind. As much as it worried him that Erin would also be put at risk, he had to admit that having her along would mean a lot to him. She would be an excellent sounding board for the challenges that would inevitably arise.

"Okay," he said quietly. "But you must do exactly what the security detail tells you to do. We will not be following the usual travel protocols. Our doubles will fly Marine One to Camp David and 'be seen' until we return. We have to do whatever it takes to remain anonymous so we will travel as support staff personnel. If any of the wrong people learn where we are, our lives and the mission will be in great danger."

Chapter 10

The next day Generals Martin McComb and Richard Newman and Director George Salazar sat in the Oval Office. President Alexander had called the meeting but he turned the floor over to Secretary Lombard after the requisite greetings and pleasantries.

Steve began, "I know it was quite a surprise when the President announced his intentions to respond without violence to the attack on our supply depot in Israel."

The nods and looks on their faces made it clear he had hit that one on the nose.

"I can assure you," Steve continued, "that President Alexander has an aggressive plan to help this shift in policy succeed. Completely unannounced and without following the usual protocols, the President will covertly travel to key Middle Eastern cities and remain anonymous until he is face-to-face with the leaders of each nation. Then he will personally present his strategy and ask for their support."

Martin couldn't help himself and blurted out, "That's crazy, Steve! They'll kill him the moment they get the chance. Even if he survives the first meeting, his life will be in constant danger once everyone else knows where he is and how he's going about this." The two Directors nodded in agreement, glad that McComb had said what they were thinking so they wouldn't have to.

"I'm sitting right here, Martin" Matt interjected hoping to lighten the mood. "I believe your assessment of the danger involved may be exaggerated. Security is hardly going to be ignored and this new policy requires my meeting personally with the Muslim leaders if we are to give it a realistic chance. They are more likely to be persuaded if I show them the proper respect. I have every intention of living to see this plan through. If peace is ever to prevail in the Middle East, and everywhere else for that matter, someone has to go first. This is a very assertive response, in some ways even more so than the ones you proposed."

"Who else knows about this?" asked Richard.

Steve answered, "Just us, Joan Hartley, the Vice President and the First Lady. The fewer people who know the details of this plan, the better. Even I will be out of the loop regarding the precise itinerary and security details."

George looked at the President. "Is there any way we can talk you out of doing this?" he pleaded.

Matt smiled at his concern and said, "Not unless you have a better idea of how to bring peace to the region without violence. Winning their hearts, minds and trust can't happen through force or the usual diplomatic process. They will come to understand and believe just how committed I am to this plan. Without my meeting with them face-to-face, the United States and its President will continue to be seen as a force for evil rather than a trusted friend."

Martin asked, "How soon are you planning to make this trip? Can we at least have our troops ready to respond if there is an attempt on your life?"

Matt was a little disappointed at the question. He finally said, "I think to do that would only serve to undermine the reason I'm going there in the first place. If we show ourselves ready to strike back at the first sign of trouble, how does that engender trust and build confidence that we truly desire peace?"

"What is it that you want us to do?" Richard asked.

Steve took that as his cue. "We will, of course, need additional agents from George's people if we are to keep our security presence as low-key as possible. When traveling, the President and the First Lady will be disguised as staff members in Joan's political entourage."

McComb almost yelled, "You mean the First Lady is going on this trip?"

Matt answered him directly, "Yes, and I really don't want any more discussion about the merits of this trip. We need to work together for this to succeed rather than continue to speculate on how it might fail."

"I apologize, Mr. President," Martin said with forced calm. "I was out of line, but I am truly concerned for your safety. Rest assured your guidelines will be followed to get you back home safely."

Steve said, "We all share your concern for the President's safety, General McComb. So let's go over the security protocols for the trip."

★★★

Later that day, McComb, Newman and Salazar met in George's office inside Langley. They couldn't believe the situation had deteriorated this much in so short a time. They had developed a great plan. Allowing terrorists to operate freely in the Middle East by strategically ignoring certain groups would surely result in violence. But then, who would have guessed that POTUS would make this absurd trip? They realized their plan could backfire by putting the President's life at risk.

McComb was the trio's military expert but he lacked experience in covert operations. Newman's career had been focused on intelligence, but both men wanted Salazar's assessment on where things stood. "It looks like we put our plan on hold until the President returns from his trip. This whole thing could blow up in our faces if we don't keep the usual lid on things while he's exposed."

McComb shook his head. "But he is going over there with the intention of spelling out his proposal to their heads of state. There will be no way to gently retreat from this plan, especially if he is successful in gaining their cooperation. We all know that his pipe dream ultimately won't work, but he's sure it will. What can we do to show him the truth of this?"

Newman replied, "We know what convinced you, General. The fanatic who killed your son struck you at your core. You understand the brutal way they think. Without a reality check that hits him where he lives, I don't think the President will see this any other way."

Salazar had an unconventional idea. "You believe we could convince POTUS by making this personal? We could arrange an event where the people affected included someone very special to him!"

McComb stared at Salazar in disbelief. "George, you're seriously suggesting we allow terrorists to assassinate someone close to the President?"

"Of course, not!" George growled. "What I am suggesting is we anonymously leak information to those in the region who would do the dirty work with the absolute directive that nobody dies while making the message clear."

George continued as he warmed to his own idea, "What if we let slip where the First Lady will be at a time when we're certain POTUS is somewhere else safe and protected? I believe that once FLOTUS has been, let's say kidnapped, it won't matter that she was returned unharmed. The President will be furious and abandon his peace plan."

"It's treason that we're even discussing this! What makes you think that you can stop these zealots from hurting the First Lady once they have her?" Newman asked.

"I know the right person to organize this and he'll do all the recruiting," Salazar replied. "If I make it clear that a huge ransom will be paid only if no harm comes to the First Lady, he won't let us down. Regardless of what happens, we can be sure that the connection between us and the kidnappers is untraceable."

McComb and Newman sat stone-faced, both acknowledging that this was a line they had never intended to cross. Both of their consciences were saying that it was one thing to sit back and let violence unfold naturally by looking the other way. It was quite another to leak security information that would lead to the kidnapping of the First Lady, no matter how carefully it was planned and executed.

Newman said, "I can't be a part of this. I know something has to be done, but allowing this to happen is further than I am willing to go. There must be a better way."

McComb agreed, "I hear what you're saying, Richard, but I don't have a better idea. George, I can't be a part of this either."

Salazar had the same thoughts against this new plan, but he also felt that if they backed down now they were no better than the cowards who declined to help his father in Vietnam. He knew neither of these men were cowards. He realized that they really wanted him to proceed; but they also wanted to maintain plausible deniability if it all went to hell. Well, he hadn't become the Director of the CIA by allowing his covert missions to fail! He knew better than anyone how to pull this off. No one would die and the President would change his mind about the peace initiative.

Still, George could see that this new plan seemed more like the work of a terrorist than a national hero. He had to decide if the ends really did justify the means. Before he made up his mind, he thought about the worst case scenario. That clinched it. After all, who would ever suspect him regardless of what happened? He decided that he alone would take the risk. In fact, knowing he was the best man for the job, he felt proud that he could do this for his country.

"I'll drop the whole thing," he lied. "I agree that it's too great a risk to take under the circumstances."

Chapter 11

Salazar had just ended his call with Ramin. The Arabic name meant a person who brings comfort and joy. He thought that was ironic given what they were planning to do. He had known Ramin for many years as a broker for all manner of illicit arrangements. Ramin only knew Salazar by his voice and pseudonym, Amir. It was obvious that Amir was highly connected in the U.S., but Ramin would never have guessed that he was George Salazar, Director of the CIA. Amir had always been a good customer, who paid as agreed, and that was all Ramin cared about.

Amir/Salazar had a long history of employing Ramin to find people who would do anything if the price was right. He typically handled the details for any job he accepted, but Amir said this one was special. He wanted someone kidnapped and he didn't care if Ramin kept the ransom money. Ramin didn't care if this abduction was about revenge or politics. He only cared that it paid well. He eagerly asked for the specifics.

Amir withheld most of the details when he explained what he needed. All he disclosed was that a high level U.S. government official would soon come to the Middle East and travel to several capital cities. He would supply Ramin with the itinerary and travel plans under three conditions. The target would not be harmed at any point in the process. The person would be safely returned upon receipt of the ransom, and Ramin's crew would inflict as few casualties as possible, with zero fatalities.

Ramin assured Amir that this was possible. He would first meet with those he trusted to develop a plan. They would help recruit the right people for the job. The call ended with an agreement to speak again after the team had been confirmed and the plan developed to get Amir's final approval.

George stared at the phone in his hand in astonishment. He had just officially committed treason. His conscience was saying it was not too late to stop. He carefully considered if he really wanted to go through with this but every time he ran the scenario through his head, the result was the same. The First Lady would be returned in good health and the President would understand that fear and revenge were simply a way of life in the Middle East. Alexander's strategy for a non-violent solution would be quickly set aside for a more realistic plan. George decided that it was up to him to protect the United States from its own President and his naive ideas for attaining peace.

★★★

Afkar was thrilled over his good fortune. Allah was indeed smiling down upon him. Ramin had said that his information came from a very reliable source. Even with Ramin's huge commission, the wealth and prestige this job would bring was almost too good to believe. This was the kind of opportunity that changed lives.

There was much to be done and Afkar would have to assemble an experienced and dependable team of at least twenty people to ensure their success. He directed his lieutenants to be discreet in the recruiting process. The target of this abduction was promised to be a very important American. The fewer people who knew of this operation, the better.

Afkar had to design a plan that would work well under most conditions. He would receive short notice of when and where the target would be in Damascus. At the right place and time, they had to neutralize the security personnel and transport the target to a safe holding area without being followed. They would also need to remain hidden while they bargained over the ransom and details of the exchange. Normally it was easy to restrain a hostage, but not in this case. This target was not to be harmed. That meant a holding place where no amount of cries for help would attract attention. This job had more than its share of problems, but he enjoyed the challenge, knowing it would change his life forever.

★★★

The Andrews Air Force Base air traffic controller announced, "Special Air Mission 1135, you are cleared for departure on runway niner alpha."

"Roger that," said the pilot of the 747. "SAM 1135 cleared for takeoff on niner alpha." He taxied onto the runway and reminded everyone to buckle up.

The passengers included Secretary of State Joan Hartley and her usual traveling entourage of assistants and agents. Under strict instructions, no one drew attention to Matt and Erin Alexander. It was intended that none of the airport personnel, including pilots, were aware that POTUS and FLOTUS were aboard. To complete their cover, the 747's call sign was given as Special Air Mission 1135 rather than Air Force One. As far as anyone knew, President Alexander and the First Lady were already at Camp David for some rest and relaxation.

In actuality, Matt and Erin were aboard the plane headed for the Middle East. They traveled in disguise to keep their presence on the flight unknown for as long as possible. Joan's office had scheduled initial meetings with her political counterparts in four Muslim nations. Realistically it was understood that once Matt made his presence known at the first stop in Riyadh, Saudi Arabia's capital, word that he was in the region would spread like wildfire. The plan was to keep their travel schedule and itinerary unpredictable. That would minimize the chances anyone could organize an attack against them. To that end, the appointments with the various statesmen had been arranged with an open time window of four days. No country would receive much more than an hour's notice of their arrival inside of that window. While this was an unusual request, many of the heads of state of these countries were keen to prove their cooperative spirit and concern over the recent attack on the U.S. compound in Israel.

Nearly twenty Muslim nations in that region were invited to meet with the U.S. Secretary of State. Many didn't reply in a timely manner. However, Joan only wanted to meet with four of them to get the ball rolling and the right four agreed to the terms and agenda.

The secret itinerary was disclosed on a need-to-know basis only. They would first land in Riyadh, Saudi Arabia followed by Damascus, Syria, then Amman, Jordan, and finally Cairo, Egypt. Matt and Joan were relieved the leaders of these key nations graciously agreed to the odd schedule. Saudi Arabia and Egypt were chosen for their leadership roles in the Muslim world given their size, economies and friendly relations with the U.S. They would be strategic allies in developing a critical mass of support for Matt's peace plan. Syria's cooperation would be essential to winning over members of the extreme opposition. Jordan, like Syria, shared a border with Israel and worked well with capitalists, socialists and communists alike. Also, because the underground bunker the terrorists built was hidden inside Jordan's borders, a gesture of their cooperation would carry a lot of political weight.

Everyone aboard SAM 1135 took advantage of the comfortable design of the 747 to rest and to minimize jet lag as much as possible. They needed to mentally prepare for the days ahead. While planned in great detail, these unprecedented meetings had been organized quickly. They knew their lives would soon be at great risk.

★★★

Matt and Erin were in the Executive Suite at the nose of the aircraft directly below the control cabin. Neither was able to sleep, even though both had tried for more than an hour.

Hearing Matt's restless movements, Erin asked, "Do you want to talk about it?"

"Which part?" Matt questioned.

"Can we discuss what I can do while all these crucial meetings are going on?" she replied.

"Truthfully," Matt answered as he turned on a light, "I'd prefer that you never left this plane. Since that's not going to happen, tell me what you want to do."

"I'd really like to get a feel for how these people live. I'd enjoy taking a tour to see the residential areas and interesting places in this part of the world. And maybe do a little shopping while I'm at it," she added with a grin.

"I'm sure that could be arranged," he smiled back. "Promise that you will follow whatever guidelines the protective detail sets? The Secret Service knows how to keep you safe, but only if you do what they say," Matt reminded.

"I know," Erin breathed, sounding a bit disappointed. In truth, she was more than a little anxious about this trip. Just the thought of it sent chills up her spine, but the risk was to her husband, not her. She hoped that showing her eagerness for playing the tourist during his meetings would put his mind at ease, at least where she was concerned. After all, she really was interested in the people and culture in this part of the world. Erin had traveled much in her life but mostly as the wife of an elected official and that had always placed restrictions on what she could see and do. Maybe touring without fanfare would allow her to enjoy her visit to these mysterious and exotic places.

For his part, Matt was worried about his wife. It just didn't feel right to bring her along considering the potential for danger, and he wasn't sure why he had consented. If he was honest with himself, he was pleased by her support and enthusiasm for his plan. It felt good to make her happy and to feel the love they shared again. It seemed everything between them had changed for the better since his heart attack. He marveled that instead of losing everything, his life included, he now had the woman he loved at his side as he took on the biggest challenge of his life.

Matt was unable to shake the recurring feeling of déjà vu that he had experienced all of this before. It was as if he had already been shown what would happen on this trip. It had played in his mind like a big budget movie. And just like in the movies, he sensed disaster was coming. That should have been enough for him to call a halt to this entire trip. However, he believed to his core that if he stayed with the plan, a positive result would eventually work itself out, in spite of any setbacks.

Chapter 12

Joan Hartley stepped off the 747, onto the red carpet rolled out for her, at the Riyadh airport in Saudi Arabia. She was greeted with all the pomp and circumstance normally afforded to a visiting cabinet member of a foreign country. Matt and Erin came down the passenger stairs with the staffers doing their best to blend in. After a quick ceremony in the airport's Royal Pavilion, they were all loaded into several large black SUVs for transport to the Al Amoud Hotel in downtown Riyadh.

The hotel was situated near the King Abdullah Palace which was Saudi Arabia's answer to the White House. Joan was apprehensive about sitting down with the Saudi Minister of State, Khazin Almahdi. She was recognized for her charm and charisma, but Minister Almahdi was a well-known misogynist. Meeting with him would be challenging, to say the least.

When they were all settled at the hotel, Matt, Erin and Joan met with the head of their Secret Service detail, Wayne Thompson. They waited until Wayne assured them that the room was free of any surveillance devices before getting down to business.

Joan reviewed with them the background she had on King Tabir. "He was born in Saudi Arabia and inherited his position. He received a business degree from Yale and was an excellent student despite living the good life that America had to offer. Apparently he understood that he'd never get another chance to move freely about the world once his father passed the title on to him. So he enjoyed himself jet-setting and impressing other young, wealthy aristocrats. Once he became King, Tabir took his leadership role quite seriously. He became very devoted to his faith and gratefully earned the love and respect of his people. He was considered to be a moderate, both religiously and politically. He would make an excellent ally in reaching out to the other Muslim countries because of his sensible position on most issues."

Matt nodded. He had read most of this already in Tabir's dossier. It was no accident that he had decided to start his campaign of peace here. After all, it was the home of the mosques in Mecca and Medina, the two holiest places in Islam. Matt had met the King only once years ago at a formal function before either of them were elevated to their current positions. Bridging the gap between their two countries would be a formidable task, bordering on momentous, if they were successful.

Matt reviewed with Joan the cultural challenges they were about to face. "The United States has a history of relatively good relations with Saudi Arabia. Your position is worthy of the respect needed to get their attention. However, your gender is cause for concern given the Muslim culture, as you well know. Minister Almahdi will avoid discussing important matters of state with a woman. His misogyny should work to our advantage once he realizes the true purpose of our visit. He will be highly motivated to arrange an impromptu meeting between King Tabir and me rather than suffer through several hours of negotiations with a female." Joan smiled ruefully in understanding and shook her head that this was still an issue in the modern world.

Matt had already worked out most of the meeting's details with Joan, but he wanted Agent Thompson in the loop to ensure his security measures supported their mission. There were thirty two Americans total in the U.S. entourage. Matt, Erin and Joan were supported by three assistants and the rest were Secret Service agents. They were split into three security teams assigned to protect the President, First Lady, and Secretary of State. When POTUS was traveling outside of the hotel or palace, there were a dozen CIA agents assigned to stay close while blending in with the crowd. They had orders to keep a low profile unless an emergency presented itself.

The plan was for Joan to be accompanied by Matt and their assigned bodyguards along with four other agents. Matt would travel in the SUV with Joan using three other vehicles and the additional agents to escort them. POTUS was not to receive any special treatment, such as opening doors or addressing him with a salutation that might draw notice to him. He was to be treated as any other assistant to the Secretary of State.

With the security details nailed down, Erin's itinerary was discussed. She confirmed her desire to see the "real" Riyadh by visiting residential areas as well as taking in the main tourist sites. She reluctantly agreed that all shopping would be done in the hotel and that she would not get out of the vehicle for any reason. Erin and her assistant, Karen Moffitt, would ride with Agent Pam Selco. That arrangement positioned two agents in each of three SUVs while following the local custom that kept the females together. The idea was to appear as if there was no hierarchy to the security of the vehicles. Erin agreed to wear a modest disguise. Pam wanted the casual observer to think Joan's entourage was taking in the sights while they waited for the political meeting to conclude.

And with that, it was time to move out and test the waters of President Alexander's peace plan.

★★★

It was late, but George Salazar was not asleep. He was on the phone in Washington talking to Wayne Thompson in Riyadh about the security arrangements for POTUS and the Secretary of State. He tried to sound casual as he asked about the First Lady's schedule. When Wayne described the low profile measures they agreed to employ, George was confident Ramin would succeed. If they used the same protection measures in Damascus the following day, it would not be hard to "safely" abduct her with few, if any, casualties among the agents.

George had already instructed his CIA "spooks" to focus their surveillance on POTUS but be available for the First Lady if needed. They were to remain out of sight as long as nothing required their assistance. He and Wayne agreed to speak again after POTUS' meeting with King Tabir.

George then assumed his Amir persona and called Ramin. He confirmed the target was expected to be in Damascus the following day. Ramin said his people were gathered, briefed and ready to go at any time.

He trusted Ramin to follow his instructions, but this was serious business. In fact, if Ramin was ever detained and questioned, George would have to make sure he didn't survive the interrogation. Salazar's conscience was relentless in urging him to stop. He did his best to ignore it. After all, the success of his plan was vital to the security of the United States.

★★★

Joan and Matt were fascinated by the eclectic mix of cultures and architecture as they rode to the Palace. In the U.S., buildings that were a few hundred years old were a rarity. Here, it was common to see ornate structures many centuries old comfortably sitting next to modern glass towers. There was a long history here indeed. It was no wonder the Arab world considered Americans to be arrogant adolescents rather than mature leaders advancing humanity. Matt knew he had to overcome their perception and bias if he was to have any success with King Tabir.

As the official convoy rolled up to the grand portico entrance, it was plain to see they were expected. There were many well-dressed men and women waiting with a small band underscoring the celebratory mood. Joan adjusted the silk scarf over her hair out of respect for her hosts. As she exited the vehicle and introductions were made, she could see the foreboding in her counterpart's eyes. Even from a deferential distance, Matt saw it too. He was now certain that Minister of State Almahdi would become their reluctant ally once he learned he could avoid meeting with Joan.

But when they entered the crowded Palace, Joan and Matt could see that it was not going to be as easy to arrange a private meeting as they had hoped. Joan asked their host in English if, after the media had completed their questions and pictures, they could be alone with just their assistants. At first Almahdi gave her the impression that he did not understand English, but then he smiled and declared that the press must leave immediately. Joan's bodyguard could speak Arabic and discreetly translated the announcement. Almahdi had told the media the American Secretary of State wanted them all out of the room. Joan remained silent knowing it was better to ignore Almahdi's purposeful misrepresentation.

Once the disgruntled members of the press had departed, Joan and her entourage were ushered into a large conference room. It was already filled with the usual political figures who attended such meetings. She requested that most of these people leave the room and suggested that only one assistant and bodyguard for her and Almahdi remain. She explained that the discussion was highly confidential. He agreed easily enough since he felt the fewer witnesses there were to this meeting, the better it was for him. He brusquely dismissed his people. Most of them stood and left without another word, clearly puzzled and somewhat offended. Joan wondered what he had said this time that upset them but she didn't bother to ask for a translation.

There were still more people in the room than Joan preferred but with a confirming nod from Matt, she let it go. The Secretary of State sat down at the middle of the conference table directly across from the Saudi Minister of State. They exchanged the required pleasantries before getting down to business. Joan knew her words and manner from here on would make all the difference.

"Your esteemed Minister," she began, "I must beg your pardon and tell you that the reason for my presence here today is not what it seems. I am here to shield a higher purpose between our countries than the agenda before us. I apologize that I could not tell you this before we met face to face."

He looked at her with suspicion and asked her to explain.

"The matters that need to be discussed today are above both our positions within our governments. That is why President Matthew Alexander respectfully requests the presence of the Custodian of the Two Holy Mosques, King Tabir, to join us in order to continue with this unprecedented meeting."

Almahdi was silent for a moment, obviously collecting his patience as well as his thoughts. "I regret to say that King Tabir is unavailable to meet with anyone today. I assure you that I have his full confidence in properly representing our interests regarding any topic we discuss."

Joan answered, "I humbly ask again if King Tabir would make time to meet directly with the President of the United States. We have gone to a great deal of trouble to make this as convenient for you as possible."

Her counterpart was now perplexed. He was irritated that this woman was apparently questioning his position and his right to speak for his King. He managed a diplomatic yet condescending, "I have already said that King Tabir is not available. Perhaps we should adjourn so you can rest after your long journey?"

At that moment her assistant stood up from his place behind Joan and said, "Minister, we are fully rested and I regret the secrecy required to bring me here safely. I am the President of the United States and I request that this meeting continue with only King Tabir and me at a secure location of his choosing. I ask that we meet at his earliest convenience. I am content to wait here until he is available."

The Minister was clearly shocked and looked to Joan for confirmation. Her serious expression convinced him to remain silent. He watched amazed as Matt removed the glasses and carefully peeled off the prosthetic nose, false mustache and heavy eyebrows. It was an effective disguise because, up to now, Almahdi had not given the lowly assistant a second glance. He also had no appreciation for being toyed with in this manner. The Minister angrily balked and repeated his position. "I regret that King Tabir is unavailable. Perhaps arrangements can be made for you to meet with him at another time using the proper channels and protocols!"

Matt had guessed it would come down to this and so he played his trump card. "I understand your reluctance to disturb King Tabir and I apologize for placing you in this seemingly untenable position. If you insist that the King is unavailable, then I believe you. I will do as you suggest by using the proper protocols and channels. King Tabir clearly values your judgment for you to deny my personal request without consulting with him. In the meantime, I will leave Secretary Hartley here to discuss several pressing matters of state with you."

The Minister looked horrified and his left eye started to twitch. He saw no dignified way out of this predicament. He could stubbornly stay with his original position but that meant a long meeting with this Secretary woman. Worse yet, to make no effort to contact King Tabir at the request of President Alexander would probably mean the end of his political career. Angry as he was, if he did as requested, this embarrassing meeting would become King Tabir's problem.

"I will see what I can do," the Minister announced as he quickly departed.

★★★

President Alexander waited forty-two minutes before King Tabir entered the royal conference room of his Palace. After offering his apologies for keeping POTUS waiting, the King turned and motioned for his people to leave them alone. Matt did the same with Joan and the Secret Service agent. He was inwardly anxious and yet pleased that this key meeting and moment was finally here.

"And so, Mr. President," Tabir began, "may I ask what brings you to my humble home under such unusual circumstances?"

"Your Majesty, thank you for your gracious hospitality. I'm sure you're aware of the recent attack on our military supply depot in Israel. Justice is demanded by the families of our fallen soldiers and my advisors urge me to respond with greater force than ever before. At first, I was prepared to follow that violent path the moment we could identify who was responsible for this horrific act of aggression." Matt paused to gauge the reaction of the King. Seeing none, he continued.

"I have since reconsidered our options, knowing we all desire peace. I realized nothing good would come from seeking vengeance. No doubt the tragic attack on our soldiers was deemed "payback" for other transgressions, real or imagined, against the Islamic world. If I were to strike back at them, they would only retaliate and the vicious cycle would continue. This is just as true today as it was thousands of years ago."

Tabir simply nodded his agreement without changing his expression.

"I have decided to take a stand and allow the attack against our soldiers to mark the end of the violence. For the sake of a lasting peace, someone has to be willing to forgive and stop the bloodshed. I am no great scholar of the Qur'an, but doesn't Mohammed - praise be unto Him - also teach that we should '… meet the evil with good behavior'?"

The King could not hide his surprise. Not only had President Alexander accurately translated the Qur'an, he had also shown respect and given the proper salutation in the Prophet's honor. He replied with a nod, "It is true, what you say."

Matt continued, "Two occasions where violence is clearly sanctioned in Islam occur when your life is threatened or when you are being forcibly removed from your home. We contend that both of these offenses have been committed against the people of the United States. Some would disagree, using clever logic. Many in this region do not recognize or treat our military and political bases as our own sovereign land. That leaves the question of our right to defend our lives."

King Tabir had never heard an American politician speak knowledgeably of the sacred scripture. In his experience, any question of law had always been interpreted according to the ways of secular thinking rather than from the truth as given in the Qur'an. All of Islam knows that the truth, as the Prophet wrote down for all, has always been and will always be. Most westerners could not understand that Allah's laws always rise above those of man's design. Perhaps, he mused to himself, there was common ground between himself and this most unusual American President.

"Practically speaking, no amount of violence or vengeance will return our fallen people to their loved ones. Doesn't the Qur'an also teach that Allah - glorified and exalted is He - prefers that we pardon and overlook the transgressions against us, for God loves good-doers?" Matt asked.

The King continued to be impressed. This POTUS may not have been a scholar of the Qur'an, but he certainly knew how to approach this difficult subject from a Muslim's perspective.

"Indeed, it is so written!" answered Tabir.

"My request is simple though my ultimate goal will not be easily reached. I ask that we make great use of this unprecedented opportunity. The United States is choosing to respond with forgiveness rather than aggression. I ask you to stand with me to condemn vengeance and violence from this point forward. Those who share in this vision of peace will urge all Middle Eastern countries and militant groups to do the same." He paused to see the King's reaction.

For his part, Tabir was trying to detect the President's true motives. There was little to lose in agreeing to Alexander's proposal. Supporting such rhetoric was needed in international politics to avoid economic sanctions and to maintain a "most favored nation" trading status. So what else did this man have in mind that would be worth risking his life to come here? Tabir decided to ask him directly.

"And what else do you request of me? I see no loss if I endorse what you propose so far, but what remains unsaid between us that will be difficult for me to support?"

Matt knew they were down to the heart of it. Saudi Arabia was one of America's closest Muslim allies but they also feared economic ruin once their oil reserves were depleted. These proud people didn't accept change easily and his proposal would bring far more change than a simple cease-fire. Matt decided to unveil his new policy of transparent negotiations and lay all his cards on the table.

"I'm sure some will see this proposal as a ploy for the U.S. to gain a greater political foothold in this region. They will say our motive is merely to ensure a continuous flow of oil to the U.S. I have also heard the accusation that we hope to conserve our own oil reserves to eventually dominate the world after the Middle East runs dry. It is even believed by some that America is plotting to subdue the world to our benefit. In all of this, I can assure you we have no such plans."

Matt continued, "In truth, I believe that the greater number of peaceful and prosperous countries there are in the world, the better we will all be for it. How can we convince everyone to stop fighting? A lasting cease-fire is the first step and America is willing to forgive these attacks to demonstrate our commitment to peace. The next step is more difficult in many ways. I propose that the leaders of the Middle East educate and train your citizens to expand into new sustainable industries long before your oil runs out. We will offer all the help you desire to set up the curriculum, personnel, and infrastructure needed to accomplish this goal. However, we must all agree to abide by a reasonable timetable in bringing this vision into reality."

King Tabir sat in silence as he considered what this President had just said. Before he made his mind up on how to respond, he had one more question. "And what do you gain from all of this? Why do you care what happens to Saudi Arabia or any foreign country as long as the United States prospers?"

An excitement arose in Matt. He could feel how close they were to an agreement. He subscribed to the adage that people who are equally informed rarely disagree. With that as the goal, he was intuitively guided to again answer from a Muslim perspective.

"I believe every soul was created to live in peace. Whether we call our Creator by the name of Allah - glorified and exalted is He - Brahma, Yahweh, or any of the other names we have for the 'I am that I am,' I believe we are all speaking of the same First Cause. In that sense, all such believers can be counted as good Muslims for don't we all seek love, happiness and truth while believing in the one Creator? If a person who does not perform their daily prayers is still beloved by Allah - glorified and exalted is He - who on earth should not be counted among our siblings? And if we are all of the same family, as I believe we are, then who should we consider unworthy of happiness and abundance?"

The King pondered this surprising turn trying to see if President Alexander had hidden anything from him. Oddly enough, Tabir felt he could trust this man, unlike his predecessors, especially when his words made sense. The deciding factor was simple. There was little to lose by agreeing to his peace plan. If the education of his people became a problem, he could easily deal with that when the time came. As things stood now, when the world prospered it needed more oil and that was good for his country.

"I will endorse your peace plan, President Alexander. I respect what you have said and your efforts to find common ground between our nations. I will stand with you in a joint effort to do away with terrorism and violence both inside and outside our borders. I wish you luck with your mission of peace. Convincing others to agree with you may not be as easy as it has been with me."

Chapter 13

It was barely dawn when the plane touched down on the runway of the Damascus International Airport in Syria. It was still using the call sign SAM 1135 to keep as low a profile as possible. While the elite in political circles no doubt knew that POTUS was personally traveling in the Middle East, the media had not been informed. After a private reception at the airport, the SUVs transported the American delegation to the All Seasons Hotel in downtown Damascus.

They only had a couple of hours until the scheduled meeting with Joan's counterpart at the Parliament Building. Matt was fairly certain President Maaz al-Assad already knew a face-to-face meeting with POTUS was on the agenda. Maaz al-Assad had followed in his family's footsteps since the first al-Assad came to power in 1970. If Syria was somehow complicit in the recent attacks on American forces, there would be many reasons for him to be unavailable. Matt had little leverage here, but getting Syria's support for the peace initiative was vital to its success.

Joan and Matt reviewed their notes on al-Assad's background. He came to power through an election after his brother died in a suspicious car accident. Matt thought it interesting that the al-Assad family belonged to a mystical Shia sect of Islam known as the Alawites. Only thirteen percent of Syria's population was Alawite with the more traditional Sunnis making up closer to seventy five percent. Regardless, many members of the al-Assad family have long held key positions in the government and military.

Not much is known about the Alawite religion. Their tenets are not published because they are withheld as sacred truths for its members only. According to rumor, the Alawites are described as believers in the mysticism of Islam including a belief in reincarnation. Matt knew a traditional approach to the Qur'an and Islam should be avoided with President al-Assad. He promised Joan he would be careful not to make assumptions about al-Assad's spiritual beliefs.

★★★

Erin was delighted she would soon be touring Damascus, also known as the City of Jasmine. When they arrived at the hotel, she asked for recommendations of sights not to miss on a tour. The concierge suggested the impressive view from atop nearby Mount Qassioun. The businesses alongside the mountain road near its pinnacle offered a cultural sampling of everything a tourist could want. Karen Moffitt, Erin's personal assistant, and the security detail arranged a driving tour of the area later that morning.

The First Lady's entourage loaded into three SUVs at the same time POTUS' group left for their meeting with President al-Assad. Erin's convoy headed north for Mount Qassioun as Karen recited interesting facts about its history from her guide book. It was said to be a place where Adam lived after leaving the Garden of Eden. It was described as the site of the first murder ever recorded, where Cain killed Abel. The guide book also claimed that Jesus traveled to Mount Qassioun and prayed in the caves that dotted the mountain's surface. Erin was pleased to have the chance to see all this in person, but her thoughts kept returning to Matt and his meeting with President al-Assad.

★★★

Ramin had told Afkar that the Americans had gone sightseeing in Riyadh so it was reasonable to expect the same in Damascus. It was hardly a surprise when Amir confirmed that the target's convoy would start their tour with Mount Qassioun. It was, after all, the most popular tourist destination in or around Damascus.

Afkar knew there was only one road up and down the mountain. That ensured the caravan would have to come and go using the same route. The twists in the road and the mountain's many caves would keep his men out of sight while still being in perfect position for the abduction. In order to have plenty of time to get set, they would wait until the target was on the way back down to make their move.

Ramin had warned Afkar that the Americans' vehicles would be armor-plated and bulletproofed. Stopping them by force would require huge firepower and that was problematic if the target was to remain unharmed. Ramin suggested using some interesting technology that combined bunker busting bombs with archery.

The sleek design of the shafts looked a lot like thick arrows or bolts used with a crossbow. In the same way that a Kevlar vest can stop a bullet, but does little to repel a knife blade, the bolts were designed to penetrate armor plating. They carried a Russian made knockout gas called Kolokol-2 and were engineered to release the fumes only after the shaft had pierced the armor. Using this specialized weapon ensured the abduction would cause few, if any, injuries.

Afkar's men were positioned on an overhang to the mountain road just out of sight of the main highway. They were instructed to fire the bolts toward the driver's seat of each vehicle. If the projectile passed through and hit anyone, only non-essential personnel would be injured rather than the VIPs. The crash barriers would prevent the vehicles from going over the edge, even after the drivers had passed out.

Afkar's men only knew the target was a woman. If there was more than one female in the group, they would have to take them all and sort it out later. Ramin would meet them at a holding facility a little north of Damascus to identify the target hostage. He would then negotiate the ransom and exchange.

Two men were stationed at the mountain top to notify the team by radio when the SUVs were preparing to leave. If any other sightseers wanted to head down at the same time, Afkar had given orders to delay them at least five minutes so there would be no witnesses to the kidnapping. More of his men would block off access to the mountain road from the main highway to ensure the same. Now they just had to wait.

★★★

Erin was glad they had taken this scenic tour of Mount Qassioun. The view of Damascus and the surrounding desert was breathtaking. As much as she wanted to walk around outside and stretch her legs, Erin had promised to follow the instructions of the Secret Service team. They knew that as long as she stayed buckled up and inside the vehicle, she was safe from most threats. The kind of firepower it would take to disable these vehicles was not easy to obtain, let alone transport, unnoticed. The Lexan windows were thick enough to repel most rounds of ammunition. The agents were fairly relaxed because they knew the real targets would be POTUS and the Secretary of State. They were all enjoying their roles as tourists even though outwardly they appeared to be "business as usual."

Wayne Thompson had put Agent Pam Selco in charge of the First Lady's security. Pam had arranged for Erin to travel incognito with a wig, scarf, sunglasses and casual clothes, similar to her assistant's modest outfit. In fact, she made sure that everyone in the group appeared nondescript so that no one drew special notice. Pam choreographed the SUVs to continually change the order in which they moved along the streets to give the impression that there was no particular importance to any one vehicle or its passengers. Going up and coming down the mountain was a little different. She tucked the First Lady's SUV in between the other two because this particular section of road was problematic to defend in case of an attack.

Pam initially objected to the trip up the mountain because of this obvious vulnerability. However, she also recognized that the real threat would be to the President and Secretary Hartley on their route to and from the Parliament building. They assumed word had already spread between governments that POTUS was in the Middle East, but none of them would be aware that the First Lady was traveling with him.

Agent Selco also knew that very few in their own government knew their travel itinerary let alone that POTUS was in Damascus. She knew information leaks were always possible, but since it was formed in 1865, the Secret Service had never had a traitor in their ranks. Pam was glad she wasn't responsible for keeping POTUS secure, knowing many people in this region hated everything about the United States. With all that in mind, she cautiously consented to the mountain tour.

On the way up, Pam was suspicious of the locals walking along the mountain road. This was a popular area for tourists and the business owners who catered to them actually lived on the mountain. The local pedestrians stared as the three SUVs drove by in a tight formation. Their curious attention increased Pam's vigilance but seeing this unusual convoy was indeed a rare sight for these people.

She watched as the city sank below her line of vision on their return from the mountain top. Pam felt better as they approached the safety of the main highway. In just a couple of minutes they would be on a six lane paved road headed back to Damascus.

★★★

As the SUVs navigated their way down the mountain, Afkar confirmed that all traffic was being held up at each end of the road. He also repeated which shooters were assigned to which vehicles. He reminded them to aim only for the drivers' area of the roofs and that the female occupants were not to be harmed at any point. From their elevated positions and the close proximity of the vehicles to each other, Afkar was certain his men could fire together and not give any of the drivers time to react.

The SUVs were almost beneath them and Afkar uttered a prayer to Allah for success. This would be the moment his life changed forever. He would be a wealthy man after today and he would have struck a mighty blow for Islam against the American infidels. He yelled "Atlaqa" and the shooters commenced firing.

★★★

Pam started to say something to Erin when she heard a sound she couldn't quite place. She looked up to see what resembled a spearhead splitting the headliner above the driver, spewing gas into the vehicle. She automatically pulled her weapon and opened a nearby compartment containing several gas masks. A moment later, a second spearhead punctured all the way through the roof painfully pinning the driver's leg to his seat. He let out a tortured yell but was mercifully rendered unconscious by the fumes.

Agent Selco knew her highest priority was to deal with the unknown gas. She couldn't tell yet if it was meant to kill them or just knock them out. She motioned for Erin and Karen to hold their breath as she handed both of them a gas mask. Karen inhaled to hold her breath and immediately passed out. Pam hoped FLOTUS remembered what to do. Putting on a gas mask is not easy, especially when you're under attack. This became even tougher when the SUVs collided. Their safety belts worked to restrain them but precious seconds were wasted as they were flung forward in their seats.

Erin had practiced putting on a gas mask only once before. Years ago she had received a brief training session on how to survive an attack while riding in a government vehicle. She kept holding her breath but was having trouble getting the mask secured around her head because of the wig. She tossed the wig to the floorboard and struggled with the mask's straps. Erin could feel the gas was irritating her nose and throat. Finally, she couldn't help but cough and then inhale. She fought for consciousness after breathing in the fumes but quickly lost that battle.

Pam had holstered her weapon and was about to clear her own mask when she saw Erin lose consciousness. The way she had peacefully gone under indicated the gas was probably not lethal. That was a small comfort but she quickly realized this was a kidnapping. Pam gambled that she had time to secure the First Lady's mask and still clear her own before the attackers made their next move.

Once she made sure FLOTUS' mask was properly sealed, Pam placed her palms over her own mask's intake filters. She was desperate for oxygen but she knew she had to completely clear out any residual vapor in the mask. She blew out all her breath as hard as she could and inhaled deeply, praying she had cleared it properly. Within seconds she knew she had failed. She could feel her consciousness fade as the small amount of gas she inhaled worked to render her helpless.

★★★

Afkar watched as the lead car skidded to a stop and then slowly veered into the crash barrier on the left. The second vehicle didn't stop until it rebounded off the first. The last SUV quickly stopped a few meters behind them and then all was still. Afkar could see no movement inside the vehicles, but the windows were tinted. He waited another 15 seconds to ensure the gas had done its job before giving the order for his men to advance. Then they quickly climbed down from the overhang to extract any females among the SUVs' passengers.

Afkar's driver pulled his van into position to load and transport them to where Ramin was waiting. Shaped charges were placed around the locking mechanisms at the rear of each vehicle. This would force the hatch doors open while protecting the passengers from harm. The loud BOOMs caused the three rear doors to abruptly flip up and the men watched as the gas plumed out. They waited just a moment longer for the fumes to disperse and to see if there would be any resistance before entering the vehicles.

Wearing their own gas masks, Afkar's men crawled in through the back of each SUV to open all the doors. The fumes had worked well and everyone inside was unconscious. The men dragged three female occupants out of the second vehicle onto the road. Two of the women had gas masks on and a wig had been found next to one of them. Afkar guessed the one with the wig had to be their primary target but he was taking no chances.

After the females were placed on the floor of his van, Afkar and his driver immediately headed for the main road. He radioed the other two drivers to load up and follow him as soon as they were ready. They confirmed they were just pulling up to the SUVs to load the remaining team members and equipment.

Afkar's driver turned right onto the main highway heading away from Damascus. The rendezvous point was five kilometers ahead and then east for two more kilometers on a small dirt road. The unremarkable group of buildings where Ramin would meet them was not visible from the main highway. In fact, it looked like a small goat herder's ranch if seen from above. There was a barn to hide their vehicles with an underground warren of rooms where they would wait with their hostages. Afkar was pleased they had seen no other people or vehicles during the actual abduction. In fact, his team had made zero mistakes throughout the entire operation.

As they drove to their hidden safe house, he was already thinking about how Ramin would negotiate the ransom and exchange. Soon he would be a rich man and would never again have to accept such dangerous assignments. His life would be one of comfort and pleasure. Truly he was blessed, but he had earned it all the hard way.

Suddenly from behind them, a vehicle passed their van at a tremendous speed. Afkar warned his driver to beware of the black BMW sedan, knowing it was not part of their crew. They both watched as the car jammed on its brakes in the distance. Then the black sedan made a quick left turn off the highway. Their view of the dirt road the car had turned onto was blocked in both directions by small hills on either side of the highway. Afkar had his hand gun ready and told his driver to slow to a crawl as they approached the intersection. They both looked left to see what had become of the speeding BMW.

Suddenly, there was the sound of metal slamming into metal as the back of Afkar's skull smashed into his side window. Out of nowhere, a black armored Hummer had rammed into their right side door violently spinning the vehicle around. The van finally tipped over sideways as it continued to skid along the road. The impact caused Afkar's pistol to discharge firing a bullet through his drivers' spine and left lung. The three unconscious women were viciously flung across the back storage area of the van. When it stopped and the dust settled, the women were awkwardly piled on top of each other against, what used to be, the vehicle's side. Afkar was already dead and his driver couldn't move.

★★★

The day before, Colonel Mansur had been contacted by one of his men in Damascus. He reported that two of Mansur's soldiers had been recruited for a big job organized by a local mercenary named Afkar. Their mission involved kidnapping a high-level American female who would be worth a huge ransom. Mansur assumed this had to be the American Secretary of State he had heard was traveling through the Middle East. He was glad his men had accepted the job and said further instructions would be provided once they had more information.

The informant had called Mansur two hours before with the details of the kidnapping that was set for today. The abduction would take place near the bottom of Mount Qassioun as the convoy of vehicles headed back to the city. Mansur was surprised at the well thought out plan since he knew Afkar had no formal military training. Assuming Afkar's people would successfully pull off the kidnapping, the challenge would be to effectively disable the hostage vehicle on the way to the sequestered hideout. With little risk to his own men, Mansur's people could help themselves to Afkar's female hostage.

He had also learned that Joan Hartley was with President al-Assad that morning. That meant the female target would not be Hartley but he could not imagine who else it might be. He gave his two men orders to allow the lead vehicle with any hostages to drive away and then kill the remaining mercenaries before they reached the main highway.

When the eighteen men were loaded up to leave, Mansur's people detonated flash bang grenades inside the vans. Both his men wore special earplugs and kept their eyes tightly closed as they turned away from the blasts. They alone had their wits about them after the grenades exploded. It was a simple matter to execute Afkar's stunned men before driving off in the vans.

The plan almost worked to perfection. Neither man had counted on the concussive force which made it impossible to see out. The windows looked like cracked ice on all sides of the vehicles. Mansur's men were forced to kick out the windshields before they could drive away.

★★★

The Colonel exited the BMW after returning to the main highway. He had been in the decoy car that had turned onto the dirt road. The demolished van ended up sideways on the highway's shoulder partially blocking the slow lane. When his men pried open the rear doors, Mansur saw the three women lying in a heap. They were not moving but he knew gas had been used to render them unconscious. He cursed Afkar for failing to safely secure them for transport. He ordered his men to be careful as they removed the women from the van.

Mansur knew they had to leave quickly before the authorities arrived. He cursed again as he stared angrily at Afkar and the driver through what was left of the windshield. They appeared to be dead already but Mansur wasn't satisfied. He took careful aim with his pistol and shot both men in the face. He grunted his approval at the carnage thinking these idiots didn't deserve to be pretty corpses.

The three unconscious females were then belted into the back of the Hummer before he gave the order to proceed. Mansur had prepared his own remote location several kilometers ahead where he could evaluate exactly what, and who, his hostages were.

Chapter 14

Matt and the Syrian President were at a standstill. Maaz al-Assad had no intention of supporting a peace agreement brokered by the Americans. The U.S. had little leverage to convince him to change his mind and Matt was running out of ideas. His intuition told him al-Assad had a guilty conscience and that now was the time to test it.

"Mr. President, were you aware that we recovered a laptop computer in working condition from the underground bunker between Israel and Jordan?" asked Matt.

"And what has that to do with the agenda before us today?" al-Assad asked suspiciously.

"Nothing as yet," Matt admitted, "but we have not completed our retrieval of the data on the hard drive. I am told there are incriminating files being recovered and analyzed as we speak. If the peace accord is unsuccessful, at least we'll be able to identify the responsible groups who will pay dearly for their horrendous crimes."

The Syrian leader hesitated before responding. "I know nothing about your implied accusations. Clearly you have no evidence or you would be retaliating instead of negotiating for peace."

Matt could see that he had hit a nerve but he felt that it was not the right time to press the matter. He resumed their discussion on the previous point, but he could tell Maaz was no longer listening.

President al-Assad was lost in thought over this new information. Up until then, he had been sure the Americans had not connected Syria to the recent attacks against them. The news about this laptop complicated his position. The more he considered what Alexander just said, the angrier he became with Mansur. The Colonel had decided to attack the American base in Israel without his authorization. Despite Mansur's assurances that Syria would never be blamed, the stakes were too high to accept his word alone.

Maaz also had political concerns about withholding support for the peace plan. The United States' decision not to retaliate was astonishing. Most of the non-Muslim world would agree America had a right to seek justice through vengeance, but they had so far declined. Rather than supporting the American's peace plan, al-Assad decided that it would be enough to issue a carefully worded public statement against terrorism. However, if President Alexander could prove Syria was connected to these attacks, it would change everything. He decided to conclude the meeting immediately. If the U.S. President did have evidence against Syria, ending the meeting would force him to disclose it. He stood to announce that the meeting was over but he never got the chance.

Joan Hartley rushed into the room with a flustered Syrian aide close on her heels. She begged forgiveness for disturbing them but she had to speak to President Alexander immediately. Matt was initially annoyed but realized she would not intrude unless it was critically important.

For a moment, he thought Joan might have word of conclusive proof linking Syria to the attack in Israel or the recent biological outbreaks in Afghanistan and Iraq. This would be just what he needed to motivate President al-Assad to support his peace plan. However, from the distressed look on her face, Matt could tell this was bad news. He quickly moved with her to a semi-private corner of the room.

Joan whispered to Matt that Erin, Pam and Karen had been abducted less than an hour ago. She added that there were injuries but no fatalities among the American Secret Service agents who had been charged with protecting the First Lady. Matt paled and could not hide the emotions running through his mind. He couldn't imagine why Erin or the other two women had been targeted.

Joan went on to say that the evidence collected at the scene indicated the attackers on the convoy had used knockout gas. She had no explanation for why all the kidnappers had been killed by a second group of assailants. That bizarre twist added a hijacking to the abduction. Either way, the three women were still missing. No terrorist faction had claimed responsibility nor had a ransom demand been issued.

Matt was in shock. What kind of people could commit such a heinous crime? Suddenly an overwhelming feeling of déjà vu forced its way through his seething rage. The ethereal man advising Matt during that dreamlike briefing after his heart attack had warned him of something like this. He also promised that if Matt would persevere in his efforts toward peace, then everything would turn out well. None of that mattered now. Matt was so furious that the man's hopeful prediction was quickly forgotten.

The more Matt considered what the kidnappers had done, the hotter the rage inside of him burned. He wanted the people who had taken his wife to suffer the tortures of hell! He wanted to obliterate anyone who had helped them by striking back with the full force of the U.S. military. What did they expect to accomplish by abducting Erin and these innocent women? Matt swore that if she was harmed in any way, he would person-ally ensure there would be no peace in the Middle East!

★★★

The Hummer with the three hostages turned onto a dirt road and dust plumed behind them. The main highway disappeared from sight before they came to a deserted ranch. They passed by a small house and parked under the cover of an old barn. Once hidden from view, the driver got out and walked to the other side of the vehicle. He opened the side door and ordered the nearby men to carefully unload the unconscious cargo.

All three women were gently laid out on the ground. Two of the three were still wearing gas masks. The third female had no mask and her face was white as chalk. The driver could tell she was barely alive. He had to hope she was not the Colonel's primary hostage.

Mansur's BMW pulled up next to the Hummer and he stepped out. He walked over to the three prone captives and surmised the woman without the gas mask was in bad shape. He checked her limbs then ripped open her blouse to further assess her injuries. The swelling and purple discoloration around her abdomen told him she was bleeding internally. He knew she would not be alive for much longer.

He wondered about the identities of these women and if any of them had been worth the risk and effort made to secure them. He removed their gas masks to see if he recognized the other two. He didn't. Mansur had already guessed the American Secretary of State would not be among them since he had confirmed she was attending a meeting at the Palace.

He powered up his laptop with a satellite modem and logged onto the Internet. He then pulled up a roster of known White House employees. Upon close inspection of the photos provided, only one of the three faces was a match to the one without a gas mask. Her name was Karen Moffitt, a personal assistant to the wife of the U.S. President. Mansur was relieved to establish that the mortally wounded woman was unimportant. His pulse quickened as he realized that one of the two remaining hostages would most likely be Erin Alexander. One of them was wearing an empty shoulder holster indicating she was a body guard. A quick Internet search for a photo of the First Lady confirmed Erin's identity.

Mansur was still deciding if the First Lady's presence was fortuitous or a disaster when one of the women began to stir. He told his men to quickly place cloth sacks over all three of the women's heads. He was still contemplating how to handle this situation, but he chose not to reduce his options by allowing the hostages to see their faces.

One woman struggled when she became aware of her predicament. Her hands and feet had been bound with tie-wraps so she couldn't offer much resistance. Her movements bumped the second woman to consciousness, but she too had been bound and the hoods obscured any view of their surroundings.

Pam knew better than to say anything. Erin didn't hesitate to blurt out, "Where am I? What happened? Why am I tied up?"

Mansur ignored her questions while offering one of his own, "Which one of you is the President's wife?"

Erin realized her mistake and stopped talking and stilled her movements. The still dazed women took in the full implication of what they had just heard. They knew they were in grave danger. This man had an Arabic accent but was fluent in English. He seemed to be aware that the First

Lady was among the captives. Who else had they taken hostage? And why didn't he know which of them was Erin Alexander? If she was not their intended target, then what was the reason they had been abducted?

Neither woman spoke. Karen still hadn't made a sound.

"There is no need to answer," Mansur said. "I have already learned everything I need to know."

"It sounds like you know very little," Pam exclaimed, changing her mind on remaining silent in hopes of gathering more information.

"I know that you are scared. I know that the older of you is the First Lady. I know that you are an incompetent bodyguard. And most importantly, I know that you and the silent one are useless to me."

Erin tried to sit up in alarm. "There is no reason to hurt us. We certainly pose no threat and we are worth much more to you alive than dead or harmed."

"You, Madame, will live longer than these other two, but you all must die," Mansur replied calmly. He motioned to the man standing closest to Pam who then smashed the butt of his rifle into her face. It made a sickening crunch as it dislocated her jaw. She was out cold when Mansur's men carried her and Karen out of the barn.

From the sounds, Erin was not sure what had just happened but she could guess. "You know the United States does not bargain with terrorists," Erin said defiantly.

"We both know that's not true, especially when someone like you is the hostage," Mansur countered. "Frankly, I would prefer to have taken the American Secretary of State. She could have given us much valuable information. You are useless and probably know fewer secrets about your country than I do."

Erin changed the subject hoping to gain some advantage. "Taking me was a mistake. The United States wants all Middle East nations to cease hostilities and work together to bring real peace to this region. Your actions today may well start a war that will be the end of you. Don't you realize that we came here to help?"

"We disagree. What brought you here today is America's arrogance and disregard for the freedom of other people to live as they choose. Perhaps you will stand trial as the representative for your country's crimes against

Allah and his people before you die."

"If that is your intention, I would be a poor example of what you speak against. I have always supported freedom for everyone. Am I really the best person you could think of to hold accountable for the alleged crimes against you?" Erin asked.

"How clever you American women are!" Mansur spat. "Has your western culture made all its females so ill-mannered? Do you really think you are innocent of the crimes perpetrated by your country against us? Didn't you help elect your government's leaders who have committed these crimes? Does that not make you complicit in their offenses? And since you are married to the head of your government, doesn't that make you all the more responsible?"

Erin wanted desperately to reason with this man. "We cannot hold individual citizens accountable for crimes committed by their governments. If we did, then wouldn't everyone alive deserve to be convicted and sentenced?" Scared as she was, Erin wondered how people like this man could believe it was okay to terrorize innocent civilians.

"It is a waste of time to discuss such things with you," he said angrily. "Take her below while I figure out what to do with her."

★★★

When the phone rang, President Maaz al-Assad was surprised it was his own private line. Once he heard of the abduction from his aide, he expected the next call to be a ransom demand for the kidnapped members of the American delegation. Instead, it was Colonel Mansur urging him to have privacy before they spoke further.

Al-Assad picked up the phone in his private office and barked, "Why are you calling me?"

"No doubt you have heard about the kidnapping of the American president's wife. I intervened in that abduction and am now holding three female hostages," Mansur answered cautiously. "I had thought their Secretary of State was the intended target, but I was misled."

President al-Assad was stunned. "Why did you do this?" he screamed.

"President Alexander has just told me some very disturbing news. He said that the underground compound between Israel and Jordan yielded a great deal of evidence that would prove conclusively who had been behind the attack. In fact, a recovered laptop was specifically mentioned. Can you tell me this computer will in no way implicate the Syrian government?"

After a moment's pause, Mansur answered, "Since the caves were destroyed, I can't imagine how they got their hands on it. But if it is ours, that computer could create much trouble for us all."

Al-Assad's worst nightmare was unfolding before him. It seemed the Americans would soon be able to corroborate far more than a shared ideology between his government and Mohammed's Faithful. Syria could become a proven accomplice in the recent biological attacks and the annihilation of the military base in Israel. He had heard rumors that the U.S. President was considering the use of WMDs in response to these attacks. By the look of him since learning of the abduction, al-Assad had no doubt that was true. It was too late to undo the damage caused by Colonel Mansur and his people. However, he would do everything in his power to keep Syria from being linked to the kidnapping of the First Lady.

What was most confusing to al-Assad was that President Alexander was here today speaking of peace rather than reprisals. Were the rumors of imminent WMDs false? Was this unprecedented personal visit some kind of perverse ultimatum where he must agree to Alexander's terms for a permanent cease-fire or face deadly consequences? The only thing al-Assad could be sure of was that this was the worst possible time for Syria to be connected to Mansur.

The Colonel had waited so long for President al-Assad to respond that he asked, "Are you there, sir?"

"I am here," he growled, "but I am thinking!"

Mansur waited with silent impatience refusing to enrage al-Assad further. Seeing the precarious position al-Assad was in, he could already anticipate what his next orders would be. He began to plan as he waited.

"First, do not hurt the President's wife. In fact, do not harm any of the hostages you've taken," al-Assad said with venom in his tone.

Mansur answered uneasily, "One has already died of injuries sustained during the abduction. That fool Afkar killed her with his carelessness.

The dead woman was only an assistant, but she was a member of the President's wife's staff." He chose not to mention the body guard's broken jaw.

"Masteje (an Arabic cuss word)! See that there are no more mistakes! I do not care how you do it but you must release the other two today," al-Assad ordered.

Colonel Mansur considered this for a moment. "I can arrange it so that the President's wife will believe she persuaded us to spare her. I can also arrange it so that you are the hero responsible for their rescue rather than being an accomplice to their abduction. If either woman dies, it will be the fault of the Americans who are sent to rescue them."

President al-Assad didn't answer right away. From the moment he heard of the kidnapping, Matthew Alexander no longer spoke of peace. His rage-filled face was intimidating even to al-Assad. The Syrian President was curious to know what Mansur had in mind, but he also wanted to remind the Colonel who was in charge. He finally said, "Tell me of your plan. If you are wrong and I end up being anything other than a hero to this American President, I swear you will hear yourself die screaming."

Chapter 15

Erin counted thirty five steps including two switchback landings before they sat her down on a dirt floor. They secured new tie-wraps around her wrists and ankles taking away any options for escape. They never removed the hood but she could guess she was not in a pretty place.

She leaned back against a rough dirt wall and wondered if the greater danger wasn't that the ceiling might collapse from age or lack of structural support. Then the smell wafted through her hood. The scent of mold and mildew in the air had probably been undisturbed for decades. She tried not to identify other unpleasant odors but an underground outhouse was definitely involved.

Erin hadn't heard or seen anything for at least an hour since she had been moved below ground. She knew there was no use in yelling for help, since she was probably twenty feet or more underground. She kept trying to think of anything that would improve her situation rather than dwell on the frightening possibilities her immediate future might hold. Her intuition was telling her to remain calm and she'd be okay. Then her entire body would shudder as the horror of her confinement refused to be ignored. She couldn't stop her mind from racing through the scary scenarios of what might come next. She tried to focus on anything else that might be helpful.

Erin had no idea what had happened to the other people in her group who had set out on the tour with her that morning. She remembered hearing Pam's voice when she first awoke, but where was she now? She had not heard from Karen Moffitt, but their captor had implied she was with them. The crushing silence all around meant if anyone was in this underground room with her, they were unconscious or dead. She cursed herself as she realized this dark reverie was not helping.

Finally, noises from above followed by the sound of footsteps on the stairs alerted Erin that she was about to have a visitor. She braced herself for whatever those steps would bring. Hopefully her captor had made a ransom demand and was negotiating her release. She didn't want to think about enduring a sham trial with these extremists. When the sound of the steps stopped, she could sense the person was standing right in front of her. From her seated position on the floor, she felt very vulnerable.

"I wish to continue our discussion," Mansur said with a tone that was almost cordial. "Tell me again why you feel you are not responsible, in whole or in part, for the crimes of your country against my people."

"That's not quite what I said, but I do agree with it." Erin was surprised at this turn of events but was relieved since a conversation was better than the other things she'd imagined. She tried to see if she could see anything of the man before her, but the hood was very effective. "I said that I'm a poor example of a defendant for the transgressions you claim were made against the people of Syria. You feel that America has interfered with the freedom of your fellow citizens. If I'm to be put on trial, shouldn't the evidence prove what I have personally done wrong?"

"This is an interesting point you make," Mansur conceded and nodded his head even though she could not see him. "You do not believe that you should be held accountable for your country's crimes or perhaps held to a higher standard than other American citizens? After all, you are married to President Alexander."

Erin thought for a moment before answering. She was having trouble concentrating with the hood blocking most of the light and air. "I understand why you might think so, but where should we draw the line that makes one person responsible for the actions of another? That's a slippery slope where a case could be made to convict everyone alive."

"I have looked you up on the Internet, Madame Alexander. I must agree that you are what you say you are, a poor representative. Perhaps the better person to put on trial is your bodyguard. After all, she is trained to kill and would certainly murder me if she had the chance."

"And so every soldier doing their job is responsible for the decisions of their country's leaders? If you were guarding your President al-Assad, wouldn't you kill to protect him?" Erin countered.

"Why do you think I am from Syria?" Mansur said coolly. "I make no such claim. However, I agree that your bodyguard was doing her job... poorly. If she was any good at it, you wouldn't be here."

"The other people who were with me on the mountain...are they okay? What have you done with them?" Erin asked.

"All of the men were left alive at the place where you were taken. I have not yet decided what to do with you females."

Erin took a shaky breath of musty air and prayed that this man was somehow willing to listen to her. "My husband is meeting with President al-Assad right now. Maybe you already knew that. His agenda is one of peace. This peace is offered by the American people even though we have suffered many recent and unspeakable attacks. My husband is doing his best to avoid more bloodshed. Do you think holding a trial is a good idea considering everything that is being done at this time in the name of peace?"

Mansur was pleased this woman was so eloquent. Her arrogance was bothersome but it could also be used to his favor. She naively believed her words could sway his opinions. That was fortuitous but there remained one awkward agenda item to resolve before he could appear to accept her arguments. "I will wait to hear the results of these peace negotiations before I decide if there will be a trial. However, someone must remain to answer the charges if a lasting peace does not endure."

With that Mansur turned and walked up the stairs, ignoring Erin's objections. He still had to arrange for the safe release of both women without being caught in the process. He also needed to eliminate any evidence that his people were connected to this kidnapping. Then there was the American woman who died. He must keep that fact hidden for at least a few days. If he was careful, he could tie up all these loose ends and make a hero of President al-Assad.

★★★

"How the hell do you kidnap someone and then lose them?" Amir screamed to Ramin over the phone.

Ramin had dreaded this call because he only had bad news to report. "It was as if someone knew our plan and waited for us to complete the difficult work before moving in to take the captives. Everything else had gone perfectly up to that point. Two men from Afkar's team are still missing. We don't know if they escaped, are dead somewhere, or perhaps they were helping the Ebn Al-Sharmoota (an insulting Arabic epithet) who stole our hostages."

Salazar, posing as Amir, couldn't believe the whole plan had collapsed. He had hoped Ramin's people would drag out the ransom negotiations for a few days. That would effectively end the President's trip and his peace plan with it. Ramin would be paid well for his efforts and the First Lady would return home unharmed if not a bit wiser. Salazar had realistically been prepared for some casualties if the Secret Service agents put up a fight, but the idea that the kidnappers would lose their hostages and be executed in the process was inconceivable.

"What are you doing to get them back?" Amir barked with contempt.

"I am making inquiries but I fear the group who did this is well connected. If they don't want to be found, then they won't be. It is my understanding that they have not yet made a ransom demand which leads me to believe they have political reasons for their interference." Ramin was glad to get all that out between Amir's ranting and personal insults.

Amir snarled, "Get back to me when you learn anything new. See if you can do something right for a change, you pig-spawned sharmoota." Salazar hurled the insult knowing full well it was a harsh offense to a Muslim. As he slammed down the phone, he hoped that his verbal abuse would motivate Ramin to fix this. He let out a snort and wondered aloud why he always had to clean up everyone else's mistakes.

After a moment to collect his thoughts, he considered his few remaining options. If the First Lady was injured or even killed, that would require Ramin's immediate death. It was critical that no connection could be made between Ramin and Amir/Salazar when the Secret Service started looking into this fiasco. Most of the mercenaries who participated in the kidnapping were already dead, but what if the two who were still missing had been spies and could talk if they were caught? Again, the idiot Ramin would have to die to protect Salazar's identity. But the timing was bad because he still needed Ramin for one last job.

Salazar's conscience kicked in with a vengeance as he remembered arranging for his CIA operatives to pull back from following the First Lady's convoy. Had he not held them back, they could have stopped this entire disaster. If they had at least arrived late on the scene when the second group of kidnappers attacked the first, his people could have killed them all. POTUS would have canceled the rest of his trip and no harm would have come to Erin Alexander. His goal of disrupting the peace talks would have been accomplished while his agents saved the day. He then considered that Ramin had been right about one thing. Their plans had been leaked and some very smart people used that knowledge to intervene. His conscience kept returning to his role in the fate of the First Lady. Who had taken her and for what purpose?

He suddenly realized that he'd achieved his goal regardless of how this turned out. The peace plan was dead no matter what happened to FLOTUS. Hadn't the U.S. government sacrificed his father for the good of the country all those years ago? If Erin died, it would be as if President Alexander sacrificed his queen to win the game. Salazar smiled for the first time in days. He had saved the country and perhaps the world. He felt like a vindicated hero but he had known all along that he was the right man for the job.

★★★

President al-Assad was taking a huge chance. He had agreed to Mansur's plan but it was risky. Ideally, the Colonel's proposal would undo most of the damage while winning President Alexander's gratitude for Syria's help in rescuing his wife. Al-Assad conceded he would have to support the American's peace proposal if only to survive this day. If Mansur's plan failed, they would all be dead regardless.

With the Syrian government's blessing, the American Secret Service and CIA security staff organized a makeshift command post in the Palace's conference room. The technicians nervously connected communication lines which were already receiving surveillance video of the last known coordinates of Erin's convoy. CIA Director Salazar was on the phone with Matt apologizing for the gap in their covert security. He explained that they dropped the ball by focusing on POTUS rather than the First Lady. Matt's heart was vacillating between intense anger, retribution and fear of losing his beloved Erin.

Then President al-Assad quickly reentered the room. "Mr. President, I must speak with you alone. It is of great importance regarding your wife."

Matt hesitated and his heart skipped a beat. What happened? Was she safe? He wanted his security team to hear this first hand but he quickly decided he could ask al-Assad to repeat any critical information to them. He could not guess what the news would be from the look on the Syrian President's face.

"Gentlemen, please give us some privacy," he said aloud as both leaders moved away from the crowd.

President al-Assad offered the first good news Matt had heard since this nightmare began. "I believe I know where your wife was taken. I have had my best agents searching for information and their sources tell us that your wife and the two female companions are being held at a small ranch on the other side of Mount Qassioun. Once the exact coordinates are verified, I will give them to you."

"Do you have any word on their condition?" Matt asked with reserved elation.

"None, but from what I'm told, the motive was money so it is unlikely they would have been harmed as yet."

"Will you allow my security people to conduct a rescue operation inside your borders?" Matt asked.

"We have already consented to your setting up this command post. Under the circumstances, and for that purpose only, we will allow a rescue operation using your agents. Do you require any assistance from us once the location is verified?"

Matt was amazed and somewhat skeptical over the level of cooperation he was receiving from this adversarial leader. He filed that concern away for the moment and said, "I will leave that up to my security detail but I am grateful for your help if we need it."

With that, Matt motioned Wayne Thompson over to update him on this development. The coordinates came in as they talked and a live overhead image of the remote ranch appeared on the largest of the video monitors in the conference room. There were two vehicles parked outside the barn, which was no doubt hiding a multitude of sins and hostages within. It bothered Wayne that the kidnappers would leave their cars parked outside and visible from above. He doubted that they were that careless or stupid which probably meant this "mistake" was part of a larger plan.

He wanted to use the X-ray satellite to scan the buildings and perform some subterranean recon but there was little time. That would require the specialized helicopter and re-tasking the satellite they had used to locate the underground access tunnel in Israel. They could not afford the required four-hour delay and a helicopter flyover would remove any chance they had of taking them by surprise.

Wayne said his people could be on site and ready to mount a rescue mission within the hour. Matt went with his recommendation and authorized immediate action without waiting for the X-ray surveillance. Wayne began coordinating with the CIA agents to form assault teams as they geared up to leave for the site.

Chapter 16

Erin couldn't begin to guess if the sun was still up or night had come. She remembered reading somewhere that being in seclusion without interaction confused a person's sense of time and she admitted that was true. She wasn't sure if the lack of contact was good or bad. She decided that having no contact was better than a beating, rape or being put on trial by these people. So Erin counted her blessings and tried to stay positive.

That didn't last long. She started worrying about Pam and Karen. All of their lives were in danger but Erin knew she would be treated better than the other two women. She started praying for their safety, but silently doubted they would ever return home.

A noise from above caught her attention. How much time had passed? Perhaps it was the Arabic man coming down for another debate. She shuddered as she considered the possibility that he had left and his men were coming down to entertain themselves with the wife of the American president. Abject fear was making her perspire and she found it hard to breathe. As much as she hated the hood over her head, it was probably keeping her alive. Not being able to identify her captors was in her favor.

Erin strained to hear what sounded like many people moving quickly across the ground above her. That meant trouble for certain. She resumed her prayers asking for protection. Then the noises stopped completely for nearly a minute. The silence was broken by a loud pop followed by an ominous hiss.

★★★

Wayne Thompson's team took the lead as they swarmed the rural farm where they believed the First Lady and two other female hostages were being held. The property was abandoned except for the two cars observed earlier via satellite surveillance. His first thought was that the terrorists were hidden and planning to ambush them. He also knew the place could be rigged to take everyone out with a bomb. He had them inspect the cars first as the most likely location for hidden explosives. Both of the cars checked out clean.

The small ranch house was cleared next. It showed signs people had been there recently, but it too posed no threat. That left the old barn. The doors were open so that they could see inside. Moving in slowly, they encountered no resistance as they took up their positions. Wayne was beginning to believe everyone had left, including the hostages, but one possibility remained. He had received intel that there was an underground storage area on the property but he wasn't sure how to access it. His uncertainty made him regret not waiting for the X-ray satellite recon before attempting a rescue mission.

His team cleared the inside of the barn and Wayne signaled to the others that it was safe to approach. They had found an old wooden trap door set in the dusty floor. It was hardly hidden because it was conspicuously free of dirt. It used to swing upward on hinges but those had rusted through long ago. After making sure it wasn't rigged with explosives, Wayne had two of his men quietly remove the door. They were startled to find a body lying on the steps a few feet down from the opening. They quickly aimed their weapons at the prone figure. Luckily, they saw the black hood and that the person was bound with tie-wraps in time to hold their fire.

As they gently and silently lifted the limp body up from the steps, Wayne removed the hood. It was Pam Selco, badly beaten but alive. She was unconscious but her pulse was strong. He motioned for one of the backup teams to take her to the medical personnel standing by. Wayne guessed they had left Pam at the entrance of the stairs to test their assault skills. If his people panicked and fired on her, Pam's death would serve to shake the confidence of the entire group. As it was, finding her there would cause them to be more hesitant in case they accidentally shot one of their own. It was easy to see the kidnappers expected them and had the upper hand for the moment. Not knowing their agenda made them all the more unpredictable and dangerous. Wayne dreaded what had to come next.

If anyone was waiting below, they would know to be ready. There was dim lighting from below but Wayne couldn't see beyond the first landing of the steps. His men would not need their NVGs but it also meant whoever was down there could easily pick them off as they approached. The story of three hundred Spartans holding back literally thousands of the enemy using a similar tactical advantage made him consider other options.

He could use tear gas to start their assault; but assuming these capable abductors had gas masks and the hostages didn't, the risk of serious injury to FLOTUS ruled it out. The better option was to use a flash bang grenade to clear the way for the rescue squad. Unless it landed next to one of the hostages, they would experience no permanent damage when it went off. That option was also flawed. The grenades use a five-second fuse and are easily recognized. The captors would see it coming and have time to cover their eyes and ears before it detonated. He had to conceal what it was until it was too late to react.

Wayne decided to lead with a smoke grenade and wait fifteen seconds for the yellow haze to start filling the room. He would then throw a second smoke grenade without pulling the pin. The people below would still be able to see it was a smoke grenade and expect more to follow. He wouldn't pull the second pin because too much smoke in a confined area would work against them. If the third grenade was a flash bang, they might not expect it to cover up in time. Under the circumstances, this plan was his best option.

Wayne took out a flash bang grenade and lined it up on the ground behind two smoke grenades. His hand motions signaled his plan to the team. They were grateful Wayne was willing to do this the smart way. Not one of them wanted to be a dead hero let alone fail to rescue the First Lady.

He then picked up the first smoke grenade, pulled the pin, and tossed it down the stairs. It ricocheted off the wall of the first landing. Then came the pop followed by a yellow rush of smoke filling the space below. The hissing sound lessened as the grenade continued bumping down the second flight of steps. Wayne made sure the next smoke grenade bounced hard off the wall so the people below wouldn't miss it. With his earplugs in and the flash bang grenade in hand, he belly crawled down toward the first landing.

Wayne could hear that the dirt he pushed off the rough wooden steps was falling far below. He realized he could drop the flash bang grenade all the way down to the basement's floor by releasing it in the open space between the steps. He pulled the pin and held onto the grenade for 2 seconds before he let it go directly beneath him. Wayne covered his eyes knowing this would all be over one way or another in the next thirty seconds.

★★★

With the hood still covering her head, Erin couldn't tell for sure what was happening. The hissing was followed by another metallic object tumbling down the stairs. She could sense that the room was filling with smoke and she tried to hold her breath. In her panic, she inhaled as she gasped. Fortunately, the gas wasn't toxic because she could still breathe and think. Then she began to wonder if the gas was a biological agent. As she considered other possibilities, the room suddenly lit up with a tremendous flash that was so bright she saw it through the weave of the hood. An impossibly loud, concussive BOOM knocked her sideways and Erin screamed as she fell over.

Her cry forced her to quickly inhale the smoke and she began to cough. She then felt the vibration of many heavy feet rushing around her. As if from very far away she heard a distinctly American voice say, "I have one hostage alive. The rest of the room is clear!" This was a rescue rather than her worst nightmare.

"Stand by... checking for exit tunnels and trip wires," said another distant voice.

Erin could feel gentle hands cutting the tie-wraps from her wrists and ankles as the hood was carefully removed. She found herself staring through the yellow fog into the faces of people she recognized. Wayne Thompson and a few other Secret Service agents were gathered around and talking to her. One man offered her a canteen of water. At first, she was dizzy and could barely make out what they were saying. She began to realize the explosion had affected her hearing and balance. Her head finally cleared enough so she could answer that she was okay.

"I'm not hurt," she managed to whisper between coughs. "I'm just dazed."

She vaguely heard Wayne relay the good news of her rescue over the radio. She was glad Matt would know she was safe. Her concern then turned to the others and she asked them, "Are Pam and Karen okay?"

"We found Agent Selco, ma'am. She was unconscious, having suffered a fractured jaw and other less serious injuries. The medics report that she should fully recover. Your assistant, Karen, is still missing. In fact, you and Agent Selco are the only two people we've found anywhere on the premises."

Erin couldn't understand why they would take Karen with them and leave Pam and her behind. The man she had debated with said he might want to put someone on trial, but why Karen? Why keep a female civilian instead of the President's wife? This thought filled her with dread. Erin was sure she hadn't talked her captor into releasing them. She was baffled at why they would let her go without holding a trial, putting up a fight, or collecting a ransom. What had they hoped to accomplish with this bizarre "catch and release" strategy? But even as she worried about Karen, she hoped Matt would persevere with his peace plan.

★★★

When Matt heard the news that Erin was safe and unharmed, he showed the proper relief and restrained elation that is expected from a world leader. Inwardly, Matt was anything but calm. He had been ready to wipe Syria off the face of the earth. He was only waiting out the rescue attempt before taking any further action. He had nearly put the world at war because he was so incensed at the mindless stupidity of these terrorists. The biological attacks, the annihilation of the depot in Israel and then to kidnap Erin while he was risking his life to bring peace to this battle-weary land was simply insane. He agreed with what everyone had been telling him. The only thing these terrorists seemed to respect was violence. The darker side of Matthew Alexander had been ready to crush them all and start over again, if anything was left of the Middle East.

But then he reflected on the outcome of the day's events. Erin was safe and on her way back to him. There were no American fatalities in her entourage, except perhaps Karen, who was still missing. At first, President al-Assad was clearly not going to support the peace plan, but he changed his tone quickly after Erin's abduction. Now the Syrian president seemed willing to bend over backwards to help make the peace plan work. With the public endorsement of Saudi Arabia and Syria, it would be easy to get Jordan and Egypt to commit as well.

Matt reflected on his near-death experience and the promise that if he would persevere in his efforts toward peace, the end result would amaze the world. He had to admit that the way this terrible day had turned out was nothing short of miraculous. The staffers were asking if he wanted to cut this trip short and return home. With Erin back safe and his faith in the peace plan restored, Matt felt he had every reason to continue on to Jordan and Egypt.

Chapter 17

George Salazar was livid. "What do you mean he's still going to meet with the Jordanian King and Egyptian President?"

Agent Thompson was conferring via secured satellite phone with the CIA Director regarding their security arrangements for POTUS' scheduled visits to Jordan and Egypt. Apparently this was the first Salazar had heard that the President's plans had not changed, despite the abduction of his wife and two other women. Wayne was surprised that Salazar was so angry. After all, the First Lady had been rescued without injury. He thought perhaps it was because Pam Selco would be convalescing for weeks or that FLOTUS' assistant Karen was missing. Still, to so blatantly oppose the President's resolve made Agent Thompson more than a little uncomfortable.

Salazar realized that he had just vented out loud to a Secret Service agent. He did his best to tone it down. "It seems like he's taken enough chances already. I would feel much better if POTUS came home where we can all regroup and do our jobs without taking such risks."

Wayne let the gaffe go without comment. "The First Lady has agreed that she will remain at the hotel for the next two scheduled stops. That frees up several agents to beef up protection elsewhere. We can nearly double the security arrangements for POTUS and the Secretary of State for the remainder of their trip."

"Well, if staying with his schedule is what President Alexander wants, that's what we'll do," George said, continuing to back off from his initial outburst. When they hung up, Salazar was as perplexed and angry as he'd ever been. He called General McComb on a secure line to see if he had any insight into the President's thought process.

"Yes, I had heard he will be completing the trip as scheduled, but I didn't get any details about his wife," McComb answered carefully.

"After the kidnapping, any sane person would have seen how futile his plans were and headed for home. I am seriously concerned about POTUS' physical and mental health since his heart attack," George said trying to calm down.

"As Richard and I said before, George, this has gone way beyond our comfort zone. The same must be true for you by now."

Salazar didn't want to chance any incriminating recordings being made no matter how secure their phone line was supposed to be. "Well maybe you're right. Let's just count our blessings and hope he's doing the right thing." George hung up and threw a briefing file across the room in disgust. Loose papers floated down harmlessly mocking him.

It was becoming clear to him that McComb had deduced he was involved in kidnapping FLOTUS. That put him at odds with McComb and probably Newman, but they could hardly tell anyone without putting themselves at risk. George knew that the President and the First Lady hadn't been close, but who would have guessed her abduction wouldn't faze him? How could POTUS so casually continue with 'business as usual' after the First Lady had almost died at the hands of terrorists?

Salazar considered what it would take to finally get Alexander's full attention. A moment later, he landed on an idea he knew would succeed where his other plans had not. What was needed was a lot of property damage and economic disruption with a minimum of casualties. POTUS would have to see the futility of his peace plan if all hell broke loose at the same instant in different locations. He knew Ramin did not have the skills or intelligence to pull this off. After all, organizing pinpoint destruction on a massive scale would require real military training, brains and talent. It was ironic that recent events had presented him with the perfect man to see this through. George would press Ramin to arrange a meeting.

★★★

The President, Erin and their entourage were finally headed back home after successful meetings with the heads of state in Saudi Arabia, Syria, Jordan and Egypt. Each of them had agreed to abide by the ceasefire pact and work together to neutralize violent factions within their borders. Matt knew the agreement was fragile at best, but it was a start.

He and Erin were resting together in the Presidential Suite of the 747. The whole world had learned of his meetings throughout the Middle East so their return flight number was officially Air Force One.

Erin had not fully recovered from her ordeal, but she put on a brave face for Matt. She was getting better each day, but the horrid memories of captivity in that awful hole persisted. She decided the best way to heal was to become her husband's cheerleader. She offered her congratulations to Matt for a job well done. "It's amazing that you even convinced Syria to agree to a cessation of violence. What a smooth talker you are! What do you think persuaded President al-Assad to go along with your vision for a world at peace?"

"At first, he was very much against my proposal. Nothing would sway him so I gambled he was involved with Mohammed's Faithful. I mentioned that a laptop and other evidence secured from the underground bunker would reveal everyone involved. Even then, it took you being kidnapped to finally change his mind. So he lives to rule another day and the world is better for his cooperation."

"Do you think he had anything to do with my abduction?" Erin asked, suppressing a shudder.

"I believe he was connected to those who actually did it. Maaz al-Assad is the only man who could have convinced them to simply walk away after working so hard to kidnap you in the first place. It was probably a combination of bad timing and the left hand not knowing what the right hand was up to that led to both your abduction and release."

"As laudable as your peace plan is," said Erin sadly, "it seems you are the only one who sincerely believes it can work. The other leaders either see no advantage to openly oppose it or they probably feel coerced by circumstance into agreement. That's not a great recipe for lasting success."

Matt sighed but maintained his enthusiasm. "Somebody had to go first and if everyone manages to keep the peace just one day at a time, this plan may yet succeed. I will take each small victory where I can."

"Do you really believe that after thousands of years of living with violence people can just forgive and forget?"

"Actually no, I don't," was Matt's unexpected response. "I think we need help and a lot of it. I think we all need a role model to show us how to break the cycle. As difficult and unlikely as this might sound, I think we need to trust each other to do the right thing. Every culture believes in some version of the Golden Rule. That's the basic point of agreement we can all build upon for a lasting peace."

"I've never heard you talk like this before, Matt, even in our early days. Can you tell me more of what happened when you had the heart attack? It was obviously profound but I hadn't wanted to press you before."

"The more I reflect on what happened, the more certain I am that it was a near-death experience. Mine was unlike any I've heard of but it completely changed my perspective. A patient, gentle stranger showed me a different world view than I've ever known. I saw the futility of the path the world has been on for many years. I was able to experience, to really feel, how others would be affected by my personal and presidential decisions. I understood the fear, pain, anger and need for revenge felt by so many miserable people. I was also shown how bright the future will be someday, but not until we collectively choose it."

Erin eagerly flooded him with questions. "You've said some of that before, but don't you think your experience was more likely a vivid dream? Who do you think the guy was that showed you all these things? And how can you be so sure of the future?"

Matt nodded his head as he said, "I've asked myself these questions more than once and I keep coming to the same conclusion; it doesn't matter. Real or imagined, it isn't hard to see we've been traveling down the wrong road. As the saying goes, taking an eye for an eye leaves the world full of blind men. A sustainable peace is clearly the better way to live."

"I'm all for that, Matt, even after what happened in Syria. But how many bad apples does it take to spoil the utopia you described? Do you really think the other nations will support your vision when the cease-fire is inevitably broken?"

"That point brings me back to my near-death experience," Matt said.

"Meaning?" Erin queried.

"I agree that it will take a miracle to stop the violence in the Middle East. If we can persevere in our efforts, I think a miracle is exactly what we'll get," Matt explained.

"Like that voice in the movie that kept saying, if you build it they will come?" Erin joked.

"Yes, I suppose so," he smiled back at her. "Every natural occurrence appears to be a miracle until we understand the science behind it. Remember the experiment we did together back in college? We filled a glass with water and slowly brought the temperature down to exactly freezing."

"I do remember. I was surprised when the thermometer showed the water's temperature was 32 degrees Fahrenheit but remained in liquid form. We figured that the thermometer was off a bit," Erin recalled. "So we kept lowering the temperature until it was at -10 degrees but there was no change."

Matt went on, "I've never forgotten what happened when we called the professor over to show him the problem. He tapped his pen against the glass and the water immediately turned to ice. He told us that all the conditions were in place to turn the water into ice but it took the energy of his tap on the glass to act as the catalyst. It seemed like a miracle, but the answer was purely scientific."

"And your point from all that is…what?" Erin asked.

"I believe the entire world is at a point today just like that glass of water. The pattern of violence appears to be unchanging but we shouldn't be deceived by appearances. I think the conditions are already in place to achieve global harmony. I'm counting on our peace plan to be the catalyst, the 'tap on the glass,' that the world needs to change," Matt said, as he searched her face for a reaction.

Erin was quiet for a long moment. "I can't figure out if you're talking about physics or psychology," she said with a confused smile. "You got all this from that near-death experience?"

"I can't explain it fully, but in that experience both physics and psychology blended together seamlessly. It was as if everyone's personal choices and consequences were working together as lawfully as math, physics, chemistry and music. I know that sounds odd saying it out loud. I guess it's one of those things where you just had to be there," Matt smiled back at her.

"I wouldn't tell anyone else about that experience if I were you," Erin joked. "No President has ever been impeached for being insane but you could be the first."

"I guess I'm lucky a wife can't be forced to testify against her husband!" he laughed. Then he sobered. "I'll keep all this to myself but I will also continue to do what I can to tip the world's scales toward peace. I was assured during my NDE that as we work toward peace using what we already have in hand, we will receive the help we need to succeed."

Chapter 18

At Amir's request, Ramin had been a busy man. Through discreet inquiries he located the two operatives who betrayed Afkar. He had also learned who they worked for. Ramin had little contact with Mohammed's Faithful but he had heard of their ruthless leader, Colonel Achmed Mansur. Apparently Mansur's father and uncle had been loyal to the al-Assad family since the 1970s when they first came to power in Syria. The sons in both families followed in the footsteps of their fathers.

Unlike Maaz al-Assad, Mansur never married. A military career was all he cared about and many were surprised when Achmed retired early. Actually, his retirement was at the request of the Syrian president, who had recognized that Mansur's talents for covert military operations were better used in an unofficial capacity. Since then, Mansur's off-the-record access to information, money and people was greatly sought after in certain circles. His reputation was spotless because he always accomplished the missions he accepted.

Ramin reported this to Amir over a secure satellite phone. Amir was much calmer today than the last time they spoke. He didn't comment when Ramin suggested that Mansur was the mastermind behind the recent biological attacks as well as the massacre at the American supply depot in Israel. When Ramin was finished, the silence lingered as he waited for Amir to say something.

"If you're thinking of going after Mansur," Ramin began again, "I cannot help you. He is too connected and powerful for me to take on."

Amir finally said, "I'm not thinking of getting even with him. I want to hire the man. Can you get him to call me?"

"Mansur is easy to find but he is very hard to speak with directly. He probably lives somewhere near Damascus. I know several people who can relay your request to him. Do you want me to give him this secure number to reach you?"

"Please do. He is uniquely qualified to carry out a job I have in mind for him." Amir hung up.

★★★

Colonel Mansur was intrigued by the message. He was sure that Ramin's connection was highly placed in the U.S. government. Knowing ahead of time when and where the President and his wife would be traveling in the Middle East proved that. And now this person, Amir, wanted to hire him to do a job. There was no reason to avoid him even if it was some sort of trap. Mansur would simply not admit to anything while he listened to what the man had to say.

Using a secure satellite phone, he dialed the number. As expected, he was instructed to leave a return number for Amir to call. Within ten minutes, Mansur's phone rang.

"I was impressed with your recent work in Damascus," Amir began.

"I was not the one who kidnapped that woman," Mansur replied carefully. He made sure to word his answer so it would be the truth. If this Amir had a voice-stress analyzer monitoring the line for lies, he should come up clean.

"You misunderstand my intentions," said Amir. "What I really want to do is engage your services."

Mansur remained politely silent. Clearly this man knew more than he was saying and he was not fishing for admissions of guilt. Perhaps it would be worthwhile to hear him out. "What do you have in mind?"

"I believe we share a common goal of divesting the Middle East of any American influence. The job I am proposing will help that come to pass."

Mansur was fascinated but hedged, "I have no interest in working for an anonymous employer. If we could meet face-to-face to discuss the specifics of your proposed mission, we might come to some sort of agreement."

Salazar anticipated this and recommended they meet at a neutral location. He suggested the Bahamas as the venue. He would appear as his alter ego Amir, make the necessary arrangements, and quietly return to the U.S. with no one the wiser. They agreed to meet the following day at the Atlantean Hotel in Freeport on the island of Grand Bahama.

George knew he was getting himself deeper and deeper into this mess but there was no going back now. He could have walked away after Erin Alexander was safely rescued, but the President seemed more determined than ever to undermine America's influence in the Middle East. If he didn't do something, POTUS could potentially jeopardize U.S. security operations on every continent. In order to prevent that from happening, the next planned disruption would have to be so devastating it would be unforgivable, even for President Alexander.

★★★

Mansur had taken a sleeping pill before boarding the flight that would take him to the Bahamas. He wanted to be well rested when he met with Amir. As he began to dream, the scene before him had amazing clarity. He found himself sitting in a room facing a man with an iridescent white glow surrounding him. He asked, "Who are you and what is this place?"

The man answered, "I am called Halaliel." The room they were in suddenly changed and became the living room in the home where Mansur spent his youth in Damascus. "Is this location more pleasing to you? I want you to feel as comfortable as possible."

Achmed just stared at Halaliel without saying a word.

Halaliel continued, "It is important that we discuss your plans for the future when you meet with Amir. Depending on what you decide, a great many people could suffer, yourself included."

"So you know Amir?" asked Mansur. "What can you tell me about him?"

"I have already met with Amir, much as we are meeting now. He will not be swayed from a violent path that could devastate the Holy Land. That is why we are meeting now. He cannot succeed without your help. Please believe me when I tell you it is in everyone's best interests for you to reject Amir's plan."

"Will his plan stop the United States from interfering with the affairs of my people? That godless country has no business dictating how the rest of the world should live. Allah has used me well to keep the American infidels from invading His holy lands," Mansur said proudly.

"I can promise you that President Alexander is a man of integrity and is sincere in his plan for peace. Despite your intentions, America's involvement in the Middle East will only accelerate. Whether that involvement is to your liking or not depends uniquely on what you decide with Amir," warned Halaliel.

"I will resist any plan that comes from the American President. I am a soldier in Allah's army. My duty is clear no matter what threats you make," he said with conviction.

Mansur suddenly awoke to find he was still seated in the jet. The landing had jarred him to consciousness when they touched down in Freeport. The details of the disturbing dream he'd just had were already slipping away. No matter, he had little time to get to the hotel before he was to meet with Amir.

★★★

Dr. Jerome Westcott had poured over the machine code for several days before he found the self-destruct command sequence that was intended to erase the confiscated hard drive. He carefully deleted just enough of the malicious code so it would not execute, let alone trigger, any other self-destruct programs.

He tried again to start his lab computer using the updated copy of the laptop's original hard drive. This time it booted up without a problem. Just to be certain, he ran an immediate search of the drive for any more harmful software. In fact, there was another backup program that would kick in two minutes after the computer rebooted. It was designed to reformat the disk in the event that the first program failed to completely erase the drive. It was obvious the laptop's owner was serious about security. Jerome disabled the second self-destruct program on the original drive.

This was the moment the NSC had been waiting for. Jerome clicked the icon to boot the lab computer off the laptop's original hard drive. It fired up flawlessly. As he suspected, a deep scan showed traces of files that had been deleted since the laptop was first made. Only an expert like himself—he disliked the term computer geek—would be able to recover them.

His forensic examination of the hard drive, motherboard and components showed it was originally assembled in Ireland by one of the big PC manufacturers. From the programs loaded onto it, this laptop had been used for many purposes. Arabic was the default language although it stored three versions of the Qur'an with search engines in all three languages. It had Islamic spiritual texts and videos that were revered by Muslim scholars. It also contained dozens of encrypted email messages that he knew would have the CIA translators and analysts salivating.

The most incriminating files he found were some that had not been deleted. He discovered three video clips he assumed came from the camera monitoring the tunnel's entrance to the underground complex between Israel and Jordan. They must have been recorded by the people testing the camera to make sure it was working. Jerome found several minutes of video showing the faces of many people and their equipment going through the entrance of the tunnel.

Using facial recognition software, he would soon identify the probable leader of the group that hid in the underground bunker. The video showed the man inspecting the camera's installation as well as everyone deferring to him as they passed. Hopefully, that would answer any remaining questions regarding responsibility for the attacks. Dr. Westcott compiled his report for CIA Director Salazar and the NSC.

★★★

This was the first meeting of the NSC since President Alexander had returned from overseas two days ago. The room was buzzing with conversation when Matt entered. The talking ceased as they all stood and waited for him to sit at the head of the conference table. Much of what occurred in the Middle East, including the abduction of the First Lady, had not been released to the media. In fact, very few of the people in the

Situation Room were in the loop on everything that had transpired over the past week.

"I have a brief statement to make before this meeting's agenda gets underway," Matt opened. "Some of you have heard that my wife was kidnapped in Damascus and that she was returned to me unharmed in less than a day. There were serious injuries sustained by two Secret Service agents who are expected to fully recover. Sadly, the First Lady's assistant, Karen Moffitt, is still missing, but the search for her continues.

"Despite this deeply disturbing event, I would call my trip to the Middle East an unqualified success. The leaders of Saudi Arabia, Syria, Jordan, and Egypt have agreed to an immediate cessation of violence. We will work together to keep any bloodshed at bay and to dismantle any terrorist groups that attempt to disrupt our peace efforts. It is no fluke that hostilities have stopped throughout most of the Middle East since these four Muslim nations agreed to keep the peace.

"We have a report from the CIA detailing all the evidence recovered from the attack on our supply depot in Israel. We have conclusive proof that Mohammed's Faithful was responsible for the horrific assault in Israel and the biological strikes we suffered in Afghanistan and Iraq. We have confirmed the identity of the leader of Mohammed's Faithful to be retired Syrian Army Colonel Achmed Mansur. Further connections between Colonel Mansur and the Syrian government will likely be forthcoming. There are many email messages that still need to be vetted. They were all found on the laptop recovered from the underground compound between Israel and Jordan.

"I'll take a few questions before we get on with the agenda."

General McComb went first. "What I heard is that Syria's government is on board with your peace initiative but may well have been involved in the attacks against our military bases in the Middle East. Can you clarify how you intend to work with Syria if they are proven to be complicit in these assaults against us?"

"Who would have thought?" Matt said dryly. "If you remember, we already had suspicions of Syria's covert support of terrorist activities before I went to the Middle East. My meeting with President al-Assad was not random but rather specifically intended to elicit his support for the peace initiative. It took some doing, but he agreed to back my proposal for his own reasons. I can guess that they are self-serving and perhaps in hopes of garnering lenience, if he or the Syrian government are verifiably linked to the terrorists.

"With that said, the First Lady's safe return was largely due to President al-Assad's help in locating her. It is my fervent hope that, despite what has occurred in the past, all the leaders of the Middle East will decide to stand for peace rather than violence. So far, Syria has turned over a new leaf and is in full cooperation with the peace initiative."

Lieutenant General Newman asked, "And what did you offer these heads of state to gain their support? It's hard to believe they would agree to your plan just because you asked nicely."

As condescending as it was, Matt gave Newman's inappropriate tone a pass knowing his answer would set the talking points for the NSC meeting to follow. "There were two major objections to overcome when I met with the four leaders. There are many reasons behind the ongoing hostilities in the region but it's my opinion they all come down to trust and economics. The OPEC nations of the Middle East fear the bleak economic future ahead once their oil reserves are depleted. So far, there is little outside help being offered to prepare for that day. Why? They believe it is because the more uneducated and ignorant the Middle East nations remain in the ways of the western world, the easier it is to dominate them in business negotiations."

George Salazar said, "There are few people in the world wealthier than the Arab leaders of oil-rich nations. But I appreciate your point about what will happen to that wealth once the oil eventually runs out. I also agree that there is little trust among enemies after so many years of deadly conflicts. That same distrust leads to fear and violence which continually feeds on itself. So we are left with a question. What makes this the best time to orchestrate yet another attempt at a lasting peace?"

Matt answered, "Have you already decided this cease-fire can't last? What better time is there for orchestrating peace than when violence is on the rise? Everyone ultimately wants to live in harmony but who is willing to go first in the peace process? We fear others will take advantage of us while we're turning the other cheek. By choosing not to retaliate for the heinous attacks against the U.S., we gained the respect of the Muslim leaders as the country that is willing to 'walk its talk.' The forgiving concepts in Christianity are also taught by the other major religions, including Islam."

McComb interjected, "But Mr. President, do you think that these Muslim leaders trust you? I can believe they'll go along with the plan until something goes wrong, but do you really expect any other nation to turn the other proverbial cheek after being attacked as America has been over the past year?"

Matt paused and sighed before answering. "No, I don't. But getting everyone to agree to stop the violence is the first step. Setting the example to prove how serious we are about peace is vital to making this work. Trust will build and peace will prevail as long as we treat each other fairly and honestly. I intend to go back and meet with the leaders of Lebanon, Iran and other nations who are still not convinced that I am committed to supporting this initiative. Once everyone is on the same side, there will be no one left to fight against."

"Assuming for the moment that all goes well and peace is maintained, how do you intend to address the long-term economic challenges?" Vice President Jefferson had long wondered about POTUS' plan on this issue. He asked the question not only to hear the answer, but also to circumvent the endless loop that was about to occur on the viability of Matt's peace initiative.

"I believe we will be asking that question for years to come, but answer it we must," Matt said with a thankful look toward the Vice President. "The Middle East cannot thrive economically, once their oil reserves run out, unless efforts are made now to develop other products and services from that region that the global market wants to buy."

Joan Hartley asked, "And what goods or services could they develop? Except for oil, cotton and some unique food products, what else do they have that the rest of the world would want?"

"Your question," Matt offered, "is a great reason why these countries are so hostile toward other nations. We buy their oil but we don't make other investments in the region, as first world economies usually do, with their major trading partners. The leaders of these oil-rich countries clearly understand they will be bankrupt once their oil reserves are depleted.

"The cure for that disease is education along with the development of new products and services that will give them a competitive advantage. I only had to point to Israel to show the economic potential they have without selling a drop of oil. More of Israel's citizens have college degrees per capita than any other country except Canada. We will work with all the Middle Eastern governments to identify the potential industries they want to develop. We can help them to create a modern educational infra-structure that will bring all of their citizens up to date in the knowledge they'll need to compete as first world economies. We will encourage partnerships with private firms who are already well established in the industries in which they want to excel.

"Remember, Middle Eastern oil reserves may last for more than a century, but their easy access to oil will start to diminish around 2040. If they begin today to make the economic transformations I've outlined, they can be implemented without stress. The desired changes will come, but their economies and cultures will gradually evolve rather than suffer from too many changes too soon."

The President stopped talking and looked at each face around the table. He could tell that most were skeptical but they were not going to argue with him. He wondered how low their lack of support would sink. Rather than dwell on that unpleasant thought, he shifted gears and asked, "So shall we get on with the agenda for this meeting?"

Chapter 19

It worked well for Mansur to meet Amir in Freeport. He could avoid being seen by acquaintances who vacationed in the fine resorts of Nassau, the Bahamas' largest city. His covert activities over the years had taught him to keep a low profile. The fewer people who saw him here, the fewer witnesses there would be to connect him to Amir's next project.

"Your first time in the Bahamas, Mr. Mansur?" said a voice from behind him.

Mansur turned his gaze from the book he was pretending to read and saw a man from two worlds. He was wearing a dark business suit cut in the American style but he also wore sunglasses and a keffiyeh on his head. The headdress was mainly worn in Saudi Arabia, Jordan and Iraq, but the man didn't have an Arabic accent. His dark complexion could have been native to many places. Amir allowed nothing about his appearance to give him away.

"I have not had the pleasure before today. Should I call you Mr. Amir?" Mansur responded as he continued to search for subtle clues to the man's identity.

"There is no need to be so formal. Amir is fine. Shall we discuss pleasantries over tea or get right down to business?"

Mansur said, "I've already scheduled a flight back to Syria this afternoon, so our time together is limited."

They moved to a private table away from the tourists and waved off the approaching waiter. Mansur, quite pleased to dispense with the small talk, got straight to the point. "Please tell me what you have in mind that could rid the Middle East of the Americans."

"Very well then," Amir smiled, casually crossing his legs with the knees together as Europeans do. "You already know that President Alexander has been traveling throughout the region pushing his peace initiative on the nations of the Middle East. If his strategy succeeds for any length of time, I fear the U.S. will gain an irreversible foothold among Allah's people. This must not happen! They characterize the proposal as offering us their western education and business acumen so that our proud nations will become sustainable economic powers without our oil. I feel certain that if we try to emulate their economic model, we will become more and more dependent upon the Americans."

Mansur asked, "And you believe President Alexander is simply using his initiative to hide an insidious plot? What exactly do you think will happen if he succeeds?"

Amir could see he was being tested but he welcomed it. "It has long been America's plan to industrialize the rest of the world while preserving their own resources and land. Do you really want our homeland to become America's pawn only to be ignored and forgotten when our oil reserves are depleted? I don't trust them and I don't believe they intend to help us. What advantage does the United States gain by doing all this? If helping us to become a sustainable world power without our oil reserves was truly their goal, it would have already happened."

Amir's answer was perfectly aligned with the Colonel's natural suspicions. Mansur didn't trust much in life, least of all the United States and its government. "Let's say you are right. What do you propose that would stop the President's plan from succeeding?"

"I believe the cease-fire would fall apart immediately if a disruptive event of major proportions happened where the financial interests of many nations would be affected," Amir said quietly, though his eyes darted around constantly behind his sunglasses.

"Did you already have a specific target in mind that would accomplish this goal?"

"I do," said Amir. "There are five essential crossing points along the Suez Canal. I have a plan to destroy them simultaneously."

Mansur almost released a low whistle. The Suez Canal had been a pivotal location in past conflicts, especially with Israel in 1967. The entire length of the Suez Canal was at sea level and that made it difficult to disrupt for very long. He knew Amir's strategy had to include such massive destruction that even the United States would be challenged to repair the damage.

"I assume the idea is to blame this incident on Israel or perhaps some western power?"

"Israel, correct," nodded Amir. "The plan is to take out five key crossing points along the canal route between the Mediterranean and Red Seas. There are two bridges, one tunnel, and two utility crossings spread across its roughly 200-kilometer length. Also, a railroad runs its entire length on the west bank. We can use that to transport our people and then add to the disruption when we make the train and the tracks the sixth target destroyed. Without the railroad, repairs will take months, if not years, to complete, depending on how unstable the region becomes as a result of the vast demolition."

Mansur was impressed. "I agree that such an attack would destabilize any peace effort no matter how much support was behind it, but what armaments do you have that can cause that much damage simultaneously? Also, are you sure this can be blamed on Israel?"

"Yes, I'm sure," said Amir. "I am arranging the purchase of a large quantity of the explosive Octanitrocubane which is 25 percent more powerful than HMX. It requires heat rather than oxygen to detonate. That makes it ideal for our varied crossing targets that are below ground and underwater. The satellite-controlled detonators are of Israeli manufacture and can be set to go off together. We are securing the fingerprints of some Israeli operatives in their Mossad Intelligence Unit – please do not ask me how. The prints should be strategically placed where forensic evidence teams will conveniently find them despite the damage from the blasts. There is still the question of motive, since Israel would have none. However, once the canal has been devastated, will anyone try very hard to find a motive before they retaliate?"

Mansur's excitement was growing. "I have heard of this explosive, although it was simply referred to as Cubane. If you have access to it, many challenges will be made easier. What about money, people and the other equipment needed for such a mission?"

Amir slid a USB thumb drive across the table to Mansur. "This has all the information on it that you'll need from me, as well as email addresses and secure communication algorithms, to stay in contact without being traced. You will be well compensated for organizing and executing this operation. I ask that you put together a timeline and budget for obtaining the technicians and any other equipment you'll need beyond the explosives and remote detonators."

Mansur slipped the thumb drive into his pants pocket and said, "I will consider all you have presented. If I decide to do this, where would I pick up the Cubane, detonators and evidence to plant?"

"I'll have the materials waiting near Cairo. That is nearly 170 kilometers from the Red Sea entrance to the canal. When you have everything ready on your end, we will set up a time and place for you and your men to take possession of the Cubane and anything else you need."

Without another word, Mansur stood up and left the table. In his mind he had already agreed to do this. There would eventually be peace in the Middle East, but it would not come from American interference. He would see to that.

★★★

Gil Kowalski, Director of National Drug Control Policy, was not enjoying his recent victories in the war on drugs. He had been focusing most of his attention on stopping the flow of illegal narcotics from south of the U.S. border. The result had been several major arrests along with the confiscation of huge quantities of drugs and cash from the Central and South American cartels. Instead of celebrating, Gil found that concentrating on that one region had only increased drug shipments from the Middle East and Asia.

He was meeting with Attorney General Deborah Voss in her office to discuss strategies to stem the flow of illegal drugs into the U.S. Gil was a man of integrity; in sharp contrast to the dealers he wanted to put out of business. His greatest challenge was how to win the war on drugs without violating the law or impinging upon anyone's rights.

"It appears illegal heroin shipments from Afghanistan to the U.S. are up significantly," he said in response to her question. "That's the region I need to work on next."

Deborah sighed and gave Gil a reality check. "Prosecuting their drug traffickers will not be easy unless they're caught here in the U.S. We have diplomatic relations with them but no extradition treaty. You can talk to their Afghan National Interdiction Unit all you want but it will be up to them to arrest and prosecute the people who manufacture illegal opiates in their country."

"Actually, I would prefer they end up in an Afghan prison, but your point is well taken. Opium has become their largest exported product. Since there are many legal uses for opium in the medical industry, it's basically impossible to shut them down." He shook his head and fell silent.

Deborah thought Gil needed a little encouragement so she suggested, "You should go talk to them face to face. That approach seems to be working for the President. Perhaps that is the first step toward a viable solution."

"I'm already scheduled to meet with officials in Afghanistan and neighboring countries in a few days. You're right that I shouldn't give up before I know what I have to work with over there. It's just that I hear the Middle East is no different from South America when it comes to government officials; welcoming favors and bribes from the drug cartels."

"Let's go back over the arrests your people made in South America. Making sure these thugs are locked up for a long time sends the kind of message everyone understands. If we can't convince the cartels in the Western Hemisphere that illegal drugs will not be tolerated, I doubt we'll have any chance in the East."

★★★

Ramin was speaking on his encrypted satellite phone and gave Amir an update on the explosives he had ordered. "I have the Cubane already. I acquired it from the Israeli army more than a year ago. I was lucky enough to be in the right place when their forces became more interested in what Lebanon was doing than in securing their own weapons." Ramin had been holding on to the Cubane in anticipation that it would be worth much to the right buyer.

Amir asked, "Can you get it to Cairo in a few days?"

"Just so! It is stored near New Cairo right now, so no border crossing is needed. Where in Cairo shall I make the delivery?"

"I will email the specifics to you," Amir replied. "For now, let me say that the shipment will need to be delivered to wherever Colonel Mansur says. So far, we have agreed that upon successful testing of the Cubane, it will be removed from the crate and packed into carry-on suitcases. It should not look suspicious to the casual observer. Also, a civilian Hummer will work best to transport the luggage rather than using a military vehicle. Make sure you have one on site."

★★★

Matt and Erin were in the White House residence after a hectic day of never-ending appointments. The living room was calm and restful, and they chatted over a glass of wine about the recent events that brought them to such a critical and exciting time in their lives, if not in history. Murray was enjoying having his ears scratched by Matt.

"Except for that part where I was kidnapped, your peace initiative is going well," Erin teased dryly.

He knew she was joking but he was not at a point where he could join in. "I think I aged a decade in those few hours before I knew you were safe. I admit that I wanted to go in guns blazing and obliterate anyone who would try to hurt you. The dangerous part was that I actually have the army to do it. I'm afraid of what I would have done if you had been harmed or worse."

"Well, I wasn't hurt, although I'm still very worried about Karen. Please let me know the minute you hear anything about her. As for the reason we made the trip in the first place, I admit that your idea could really work. Offering to be the first country to rise to the best that is within us and setting a peaceful example will go a long way toward proving your sincerity. The U.S. has been hit hard this past year and the leaders over in the Middle East know my abduction made it all very personal for you. It's easy to believe that you will strike back with a vengeance at the first sign of trouble."

Matt shook his head as he marveled that those awful events actually ended up supporting his intended goal. "It sure does seem like a lot of lucky breaks turned all those bad situations to our advantage.

"When I go back, I will miss your pep talks at the end of the day. I may call just to hear your voice. I apologize in advance if I forget the time difference," he said as he touched her cheek. "I don't know if I could have done all this without you." Matt could feel himself getting a little choked up. They had surprised each other in how hard they both worked to heal their relationship. Together, they had accomplished much more than a ceasefire. Their love was now stronger than ever because they knew it would endure.

"Promise me something?" Erin asked.

"And what would that be?"

"Promise me you'll wait at least 24 hours before you make a decision to respond in kind to any violence that may happen in the Middle East from here on?" Her expression and tone said clearly how important she thought this was.

Matt started feeling the same déjà vu experience as before. He could vaguely remember seeing this exact scene between them unfolding just as it was now. He remembered watching it like a movie being played for him during his near-death experience. He sensed that it was important for him to agree to Erin's request. He also knew that he was going to be tested on this promise in the near future.

After considering this for what seemed like a long time, he finally answered her. "Yes, I will wait a day before I make any such decisions. I already know I'll have to reach beyond my depth to maintain enough patience and trust when the time comes to keep this promise."

Erin leaned over to kiss him. Murray trotted off to his dog bed and settled down for the evening.

Chapter 20

Ramin had never wanted to meet Achmed Mansur, let alone do business with him. His reputation as a merciless killer was well deserved and now Amir had hired this ruthless patriot to do his dirty work. Ramin desired to get this transaction over with as quickly as possible.

Colonel Mansur was impressed with Amir's plan to immobilize the Suez Canal. His greatest reservation in accepting this mission was acquiring and using the Cubane. He knew Cubane was perfect for this mission, but only Ramin had any for sale. Making matters worse, the idiot knew nothing about the high-tech explosive.

That presented another problem. No one was sure how much Cubane was needed to destroy their intended targets. Mansur appreciated the irony of trying to keep a low profile while testing such a powerful explosive. He often employed the same trusted demolitions expert but the man had never before worked with Cubane. Rather than hire someone he didn't know, Mansur had to trust that his expert could safely carry out the test.

Another concern was that people might see the test detonation, even though they were miles from the nearest town. They decided it would be better to do this at night. While the explosion would be seen from a greater distance after sunset, anyone investigating the blast would not easily track where the test took place or where they went after it was over.

Ramin's warehouse was several kilometers away from the test site and had long ago become a useless building for any kind of real commerce. Its original purpose had been as a staging area for the people and equipment used to pave roads connecting New Cairo with Cairo and Alexandria. Once the highways had been completed, the construction company was glad to sell the property, cheap. Its remote location was perfect for Ramin's needs.

Mansur had ordered his people to prepare a deep hole to safely test the explosive. The pit was perhaps five meters deep by two meters wide. It would force the explosion skyward and protect them from the concussive blast. The fireball would be noticeable for a few seconds but there was little they could do about that. Since the Cubane had remained in his warehouse for a year without incident, Ramin was sure it was safe to sell. But would it perform as advertised?

The explosives expert carefully fashioned the Cubane into a sphere a little larger than a squash ball. The detonators used for this product were specifically designed to generate enough heat to cause the Cubane to ignite without requiring oxygen. That was one of the unique features of this substance. It would blow objects up under water as well as below ground or even in outer space.

Though it wasn't very high tech, the demolitions expert wrapped duct tape around the Cubane and detonator and lowered both down to the bottom of the hole with a long length of string. The substance was supposed to be quite stable but old and careful habits die hard. No self-respecting explosives specialist would simply toss a bomb into a deep hole, no matter how stable the Cubane was supposed to be.

Once it was in place, the group of men retreated to a distance of about 100 meters to begin the experiment. The detonator was satellite radio controlled. Ramin handed the trigger device to Mansur, absolving himself of any responsibility for the test. Mansur didn't hesitate. He smiled as he lifted the cover guard and pressed the detonation button with a flourish. For a moment, nothing happened. The expert started to offer an explanation for the delay when a tremendous explosion shot flames far into the night sky. A moment later, sand particles began to rain down upon them. They burned like pin pricks as it touched their exposed skin. The falling grains of sand had become small droplets of molten glass from the heat of the blast.

None of the observers had ever seen such a powerful display from such a small quantity of explosive. Mansur was impressed and pleased as he reached for his satellite phone. Because this call had been prearranged, Amir picked up immediately.

"Did you test the Cubane?" Amir asked.

"We just did. Everything seems to be in order," was Mansur's short reply. "You can pay this man his money," and he hung up.

Both Mansur and Ramin yelled for their men to prepare to leave. As everyone rushed to pack up their gear, Mansur reflected on his disgust for men like Ramin. He hated cowards who profited from worthy causes but were afraid to get their hands dirty. Such men only believed in money and were no better than the infidels.

Ramin despised Mansur knowing he was responsible for killing Afkar and his team. After executing so many good men, he had released the hijacked hostages without receiving a ransom. It was as if Mansur was working for the Americans. Only a crazy man would do that.

★★★

Gil Kowalski did not feel at home in the hot, dry climate of Afghanistan. His counterpart in the Afghan government, Wajid, feigned an interest in what Gil had to say. This American would never understand the pressures of living in this part of the world. "He speaks of stopping the flow of illegal drugs into America but what do I care about that?" he thought with a frown.

Afghanistan is the largest global supplier of opiates to the medical profession and Wajid knew it had become one of their largest and most profitable exports. He hated that America wanted countries like his to take on the inherent risks of manufacturing opiates but complained loudly when some of it was used illegally.

Still, he wanted to maintain good relations between his government and the United States. Rather than divulge the identities of any illicit opium manufacturers in his country, he hoped to offer other information that would make this man go away happy. As Gil spoke on at length, Wajid appeared to be taking notes on his laptop. What he was actually doing was scanning intelligence reports of criminal activity throughout his country.

Finally, he landed on a suspicious activity memo that looked very promising. It was nothing definitive but the implications of the memo became the distraction he'd been looking for. Apparently, someone was offering an impressive fee for a dangerous assignment that would last about a week and required travel to Egypt. To recruit talent from as far away as Afghanistan could mean many things and none of them were good. Knowing of America's current push for peace in the Middle East, Wajid suspected this memo would divert Gil from his opium witch hunt.

"Do you mean to say that mercenaries in this region are being recruited to work in Egypt?"

Wajid replied, "To hear that someone is hiring mercenary talent is not so unusual. However, that they are only needed for a short time and will travel to Egypt is very much out of the ordinary."

"Would you hazard a guess as to the kind of work you think they'll do in Egypt?"

"It could be anything from the personal protection of one man to an entire military operation. Given the short amount of time they are needed, a military operation is likely. I also find it interesting that they are looking for men who do not live where the job will take place. That implies that they don't want anyone available for questioning after the assignment is done."

Gil's membership in the NSC put him in a unique position to understand the significance of this news. He quickly concluded the meeting with Wajid and excused himself. He needed to return to the American Embassy and pass the information along without delay. He didn't know how much he could trust the validity of the intelligence from Wajid but this was big enough that he couldn't ignore it.

★★★

The chief of CIA operations in Kandahar was Tom Strickland. He sat patiently listening to Gil describe his conversation with the head of Afghanistan's Counter-Narcotics Department. Like Gil, Tom didn't know how much they could trust the intel Wajid had provided, but he promised Gil he would run the information past his colleagues. Perhaps they could link this with other fragments of intelligence to make sense of it all.

Tom's first call was to Isaac, an old friend who worked for Mossad. The man worked from behind a desk these days, but he still kept up with the hot issues at any given moment. When Isaac picked up, they spent a few minutes catching up on their personal lives. When the pleasantries were out of the way, Tom asked, "What do you know about someone hiring mercenaries in Afghanistan for a short-term job in Egypt?"

Isaac answered slowly with another question, "Where did you hear that?"

Tom mentioned the ever growing chain of sources for the information and admitted it might be nothing more than rumors, given the route this intel took to get to him.

"I'm going to do some checking around here but, if this connects with some other recent events, I think the answer will be beyond both our pay grades," Isaac said.

"That doesn't surprise me, though the tip came from a member of our National Security Council," said Tom. "What do you know about this that we don't?"

Isaac's voice lowered as he said, "It's been nice talking with you, Tom. If I have anything I can tell you, I'll be in touch."

Tom knew better than to ask for more details at that point. He said goodbye and hung up.

★★★

Isaac walked straight into Moshe's office. Moshe was a Senior Field Agent with the ongoing assignment of monitoring any security threats arising out of Egypt. When Isaac told him of the rumored mission in Egypt, they both stared at each other. Isaac was aware that their agents had observed something quite disturbing just the night before in the desert east of New Cairo. In light of the U.S. President's peace initiative in the Middle East, he thought the recruitment of mercenaries in Kandahar for a job in Egypt might be related.

Isaac asked, "Do you think mercenaries were responsible for that explosion your agents saw in the desert last night?"

"Yes. The timing and nature of the incident coincides only too well with an embarrassing theft that occurred about a year ago." Moshe started at the beginning. "Our scientists were experimenting with a new explosive called Cubane. It was originally developed in America but they kept the formula to themselves. Apparently, it releases far greater energy per gram than Semtex or even HMX and it's just as stable."

Isaac asked, "So they had this Cubane for over a year but hadn't used it yet?"

Moshe said, "That part didn't surprise us. The stolen batch was dangerous. The damn stuff was so unstable that it would blow up when dropped from just a few meters. We assumed whoever had taken it figured that out and quietly got rid of it."

Isaac said, "That's why we didn't tell anyone about the theft! So those idiots don't know it's unstable?"

Moshe nodded as he replied, "That's what we thought, but it appears we were wrong. By the way, the unstable Cubane tested with a much greater explosive force than the improved mixture we have today. Regardless, it disappeared along with the special detonators our team developed to ignite it remotely by an encrypted satellite signal."

Isaac interjected, "Did you find out who took it or where it was located?"

Moshe smiled, "We got lucky. We still don't know for sure who stole it or how, but we do know who ended up with it. A sleazy arms dealer named Ramin Acaba has it in a remote warehouse in Egypt. Last night, our two surveillance operatives who covertly witnessed that test explosion near New Cairo were able to track it down. They also confirmed the quantity they have is enough to level an entire city block in downtown Tel Aviv."

Isaac started to put it all together, "So you have the recruitment of mercenaries from Afghanistan for a job in Egypt, where you know this unstable Cubane was just tested after lying idle for a year. There is also the timing of the U.S. President's peace initiative with the Egyptian government. These details isolated from each other don't mean much. Together they spell big trouble and we don't have a lot of time to react."

Moshe shook his head. "We still don't know the terrorists' target and Mossad can't announce this discovery without conceding responsibility for the stolen Cubane. That's embarrassing enough but no one will want to admit that we conduct covert surveillance inside of Egypt. Our wisest course is to turn what we know over to the Americans and let them deal with it."

"So should I inform my contact with the CIA?" Isaac asked.

"No! We must follow our chain of command and then communicate from one government head to another. I'll call my supervisor in Tel Aviv. The CIA may wind up with this eventually, but we can't start with them. No one in Mossad will want to take the blame for this mess, but there's too much at stake to not do our part to stop it."

★★★

Moshe kept moving higher and higher up the Mossad hierarchy, with the information that he had gathered. He was kicked upstairs each time because none of his superiors saw an advantage to becoming involved. He finally told his story to the Director of Mossad. He too did not want to be the one to bring this to Egypt's attention. However, the eminent danger, to so many, could not be ignored. He gave Moshe permission to break the chain of command and unofficially contact the head of security for the United States. That way, the number of people who knew about this would be kept to a minimum. Also, Israel's government could deny having direct knowledge, if the situation literally blew up later on.

Moshe's next call was to DNI Director Richard Newman in Washington. It took a while, but he confirmed to each new person that he had information regarding a massive terrorist attack being prepared in Egypt. Finally, his call was put through.

"Newman here. They tell me you're calling from Mossad with a report of possible terrorist activities in Egypt?"

"Yes sir, though unofficially!" Moshe replied, and he proceeded to describe the known high points of the possible threat, off the record, to the Director.

Newman surmised that George Salazar was somehow behind this despite his promise to drop any plans to disrupt POTUS' peace initiative. Newman had to do his job and that included notifying President

Alexander of this potential threat to the tenuous balance of peace in the Middle East. He would consult with General McComb later regarding what should be done about Salazar.

Chapter 21

"I apologize for the short notice of this NSC meeting," began President Alexander. "It couldn't be helped. I'll let Director Newman fill you in on the latest."

Newman looked at Salazar before speaking. A moment passed between them, as they assessed what the other person knew. Salazar held his gaze steady even though he could guess this wasn't going to be good.

"Our friends in Mossad called me unofficially to offer a heads-up on a possible Middle East terrorist attack. We don't yet know where or when, but we do know that the most powerful explosive short of nuclear weapons, Octanitrocubane, also known as Cubane, will be used. We believe that the intended target is in or near Egypt. All signs point to the terrorists striking in the next few days."

The President added, "We have already alerted the Egyptian government to this potential attack. Because of our mutual agreement to fight terrorism in the Middle East, they are allowing a specialized American team to coordinate with the Egyptian authorities in stopping this threat."

Salazar decided his best defense was to take on a high profile. He asked Director Newman, "How does Mossad know this? And why are they so sure the terrorists are going to use this super explosive, you called it Cubane?"

Newman looked directly at him for a long second before responding. "Apparently, the Cubane was stolen from the Israelis about a year ago. It was by luck that two of their agents witnessed an explosion last night, most likely a test, about five miles east of New Cairo. They dropped everything and arrived near the scene in time to take pictures of the people getting into their vehicles to leave. Their night vision telephoto lens was able to take some clean photos. As the suspects left the scene, they went in two different directions. The Mossad agents decided to follow the larger group hoping they had the explosives with them. It appears to have been a good guess.

"That group ended up at a remote warehouse owned by a known arms dealer named Ramin Acaba. The agents took up a position outside the warehouse at a discreet distance. Using high-powered scopes, they were able to identify the original Hebrew warning that the crate contained Cubane. They are keeping the warehouse under surveillance, but so far the Cubane has not been moved. Before you ask, this is the first we've heard that the Israelis had lost such a large quantity of the compound."

Salazar asked, "Just how much of it was taken?"

Newman didn't bother to look at him as he responded. "Mossad admits that Ramin Acaba has enough Cubane to destroy pretty much any target we can imagine. Since the test was conducted near New Cairo, we're guessing the target is likely to be in northern Egypt.

Undaunted, Salazar asked a follow-up question. "You said the Cubane is still being stored at the warehouse location? If so, it sounds like we can stop this attack before it starts."

Newman explained, "We can't guarantee that it's still there but the Mossad agents on the scene believe that it is. They watched as it was carefully separated and packed into small suitcases. Those cases were then stored in a large SUV that is still parked inside the warehouse in full view of the agents' surveillance position.

"The terrorists will reveal the general direction of their intended target, once they exit the property. There's only one highway nearby. Turning right will take them to Alexandria while a left turn will take them to Cairo. If we go in before they attempt to transport the Cubane, we'll only have them on an illegal weapons charge instead of conspiracy. The area surrounding the warehouse is not populated and it's as good as it gets for taking them down, while risking as few casualties as possible.

Salazar had one more question. "And we believe this Acaba character is the one planning the attack?"

"We believe Ramin Acaba is the seller of the Cubane, which is a major crime. However, we want to get the buyer, too. Facial recognition software, of the stills the Mossad agents provided from the test site, has identified retired Syrian Colonel Achmed Mansur as the number one suspect."

Matt took the floor again. "I am authorizing our top Delta Force team to coordinate this mission with their Egyptian counterparts. Our people will take the lead and the risk. Egypt is not aware of Mossad's involvement thus far, so they probably believe our intel is coming through American channels. I have not lied to the Egyptian President about this, but neither do I want anyone volunteering the information, if the question does not come up. I believe a policy of honesty and transparency is the best way to maintain the trust we'll need to build upon for the future. However, for the Egyptians to learn that the Israelis are currently conducting covert surveillance on their soil is asking too much too soon, in gaining their cooperation."

Matt did not feel good about this omission of information to the Egyptian government. He would remember to discuss this integrity issue with Erin, his worthy advisor on questions of moral conscience. For now, he was choosing to be "wise as serpents yet harmless as doves."

He turned the meeting over to the NSC members and left for a pressing appointment in the Oval Office. He knew he could trust these intelligent people to develop a plan that would minimize the damage intended by the terrorists.

★★★

As Matt walked past the same chair he collapsed in during his heart attack, the familiar déjà vu feeling washed over him. He sat down and closed his eyes for a moment. The memory of that strange briefing returned and he recalled that this situation in Egypt was a major focus of discussion with the man in iridescent white. He had been told that if everything unfolded correctly up to this point, the success of his peace plan hinged on what they collectively did about this new terrorist threat.

For just a moment, Matt found himself reliving a portion of that experience with amazing clarity. The man had suggested two additions to the

Delta Force team that seemingly made no sense. Both were archeologists who trained at Harvard; one American and one originally from Egypt. Matt didn't know either man but he now clearly recalled their names: Dr. Mark Heston and Dr. Nuri Zayd. He remembered that it was of the utmost importance to include these two men as consultants to the team in Egypt. He couldn't remember why but Matt knew their presence would be vital to the success of his peace initiative.

★★★

It took a moment for the NSC members to realize POTUS was back. He stood quietly in the doorway reviewing what he was about to say. The various discussions trailed off and they turned respectfully to see why he had returned. Matt spoke to Richard Newman directly. "I want you to add two civilians to the Delta Force team as advisors. They are Doctors Mark Heston and Nuri Zayd. They work for Harvard but are currently in Egypt doing research at the University of Cairo."

Newman asked, "Mr. President, what kind of doctors are you adding to the team?"

"They're archeologists."

"Uh, yes Sir. And what if they refuse?" he asked, clearly puzzled by this unusual directive.

Matt smiled and walked away with a confident, "If anyone can persuade them, it's you. Call them and set it up right away."

It was not the first time President Alexander had baffled everyone in the room. It wasn't even the first time they failed to see good reasoning behind his thinking. And the addition of two archeologists to a covert operations team, even as advisors, was by any measure nonsensical. However, as long as the two doctors agreed to follow the ops leader's instructions, there was no good reason to object to them being a part of the team.

Newman made a note of the names and continued on with the briefing.

★★★

Mark and Nuri were indeed archeologists conducting research at the University of Cairo. They met each other a decade before during their graduate years at Harvard. They were both working to translate the hiero-glyphics found on ancient artifacts at various excavation sites throughout Egypt. When Lieutenant General Newman's assistant contacted them with instructions to call him back on a secured line from the nearby American Embassy, they didn't know what to think.

An hour later, they were surprised when everyone at the Embassy was expecting them. They had suspected this was some prank being pulled by one of the graduate students. Soon they found themselves in the office of the U.S. Ambassador to Egypt speaking on a secure line to Director Newman. The Ambassador stepped out of the room and closed the door.

"Gentlemen," Newman began, "the team leader in Cairo will be able to share more details about this grave situation once you both agree to come on board. Confidentiality is paramount. Let me say that President Alexander has personally asked that you two join a special team to help stop a terrorist act on Egyptian soil."

The scientists just sat there in stunned silence. Newman realized he would have to provide more information for the gravity of the situation to be understood.

"We don't know the exact target but it is conceivable that one or more of Egypt's ancient treasures is at risk. The potential threat may be against the Cairo Museum, or perhaps some treasured antiquities in Alexandria. We really don't know as yet. The point is that we need your expertise and advice and especially your presence as we work to thwart this terrorist plot."

Mark was the first to speak, "You said the President asked for us by name? I've never met the President and I sure didn't vote for him. Who are you really?"

Nuri had gathered his wits enough to add, "I guess I don't get the joke. I really don't think this is funny. Can we get back to work now?"

Newman knew this was not an easy story to believe. He regretted leading with "the President asked for you by name." He tried to redeem his credibility after such a faulty start.

"I assure you this is no joke. I was serious when I said Egypt is facing an imminent terrorist attack and that we need your particular expertise on the team assigned to stop them. If you agree to help us, I will make sure that your supervisor at the University agrees to grant you a short and immediate sabbatical."

Mark asked, "Is this dangerous? I mean, could we be hurt or worse if we decide to help you?"

Newman answered indirectly by promising that every precaution would be taken to ensure their safety. He added that if these terrible events were not prevented, the lives of many innocent people in Egypt would be threatened, including their own. Bowing to the pressure, they both reluctantly agreed to join the team.

Chapter 22

Newman had asked General McComb to meet with him after he had spoken to the two archeologists. McComb was reluctant because he could guess what was coming and he wanted nothing to do with Salazar and his schemes. He finally agreed to take a walk with Newman around Lafayette Park.

McComb opened by trying to steer the conversation away from Salazar. "So why did POTUS add those two archeologists to the Delta Force team?"

"I have no clue what that was about," Newman said with frustration. "If he hadn't given their full names and said to contact them at Cairo University, I would have thought he was kidding. As it stands, they have agreed to help. But you know I didn't ask you out here to talk about them."

McComb sighed and asked, "All right then. What's George done now?"

Newman said, "I believe he has gone ahead with his own agenda to disrupt the President's peace initiative. This latest threat out of Egypt has his markings all over it. At least he's been warned that everyone, including Mossad and the Egyptian government, is aware of the plan."

"Don't be so sure that will stop him," McComb said with alarm. "If Salazar is behind this, he can guide the terrorists through that minefield as long as no one is positive of their exact target."

Newman added, "There was something I didn't say in that briefing that's very important. The President insisted that I leave out this vital piece of information."

"Do I want to know?" McComb asked cautiously.

Newman explained, "The Cubane these terrorists have is a defective batch that is less than stable. Apparently it can blow up just from being dropped or shaken too hard. They've obviously been lucky so far, but how long will that last?"

McComb asked, "And you're saying the people who have it now aren't aware of this?"

Newman hesitated but nodded, "That's a reasonable assumption. No one in their right mind transports unstable explosives over unpaved roads. That test they held in the Egyptian desert was probably to measure its destructive power. They wouldn't have known to test it for stability."

McComb saw this development could be both good and bad. "POTUS insisted that you withhold that information at the NSC meeting? He obviously suspects information leaks. The good news is that he probably doesn't suspect you since you brought this to him."

Newman shook his head. "You didn't see his face when he gave that order. It was as if he knew I was somehow involved and was giving me a chance to make amends."

"You are not the only one he suspects since he kept the information from the rest of the NSC. That is cause for concern, but POTUS can't prove anything against us unless Salazar talks," McComb reminded him. "Regardless, it sounds like the Delta Force team has this situation covered. Is the Cubane really so unstable that these terrorists can blow themselves up driving down a bumpy road?"

Newman nodded this time. "That could happen, but the plan is to keep them on paved roads. As soon as we know whether they are headed toward Cairo or Alexandria, Delta Force will take them down before they get to any inhabited areas."

"That sounds logical to me," said McComb. "Even if the Cubane ignites, there would be limited casualties. Just how much jostling is needed to set it off?"

"The risk of an explosion was described to me as being something like the structural integrity of an egg. The shape of an egg can take a lot of pressure without breaking, if applied correctly. But dropping one off a counter will break it every time. Because the Cubane was carefully packed inside those small suitcases, it shouldn't blow up unless dropped several feet onto a hard surface or somehow sharply impacted.

"It would take something with the force of a car wreck or throwing it off the truck to accidentally set it off. You heard that Mossad believes they know where the stuff is and they are not taking their eyes off it."

McComb said confidently, "We won't be connected to this no matter what happens in Egypt. Let the Delta Force team do what they're trained to do."

"But what if they catch up with Salazar and he tells them we're involved?" Newman exclaimed.

"I would keep him out of the loop as much as you can and have nothing more to do with him," McComb warned.

"But he reports to me and can effectively end our careers regardless of proof," Newman said. "With all his connections, he won't stay in the dark for long."

A thought occurred to McComb that could resolve the whole mess. "Why don't you tell Salazar that you want him in the Middle East to personally oversee the CIA's covert operations in these precarious times? He might just end up in the wrong place at the right time. Either he blows up with the terrorists or they take him out after discovering the Cubane is defective."

"That's a devious idea. And I can live with it. It gets Salazar out of the way and allows him to lie in the bed he's already made."

★★★

"What do you mean you want me to go to Egypt?" George Salazar bellowed. Lieutenant General Newman was his boss but George was livid. Newman obviously intended to put him in harm's way.

Newman pulled him up short, "I mean it George. You will leave for Cairo at once. There is a lot of confusion going on in Egypt right now that I think you are uniquely qualified to resolve. If anyone can keep a lid on the current terrorist activities over there, it's you."

Salazar considered this for a moment and he read between the lines. He had no leverage against Newman that didn't take himself down as well. He thought Newman was a coward for not following through with their original intentions, but what was to be done now?

He considered whether or not his presence in Cairo would change anything. It wouldn't if everything went according to plan and he would be in a better position to keep things moving forward, if Mansur couldn't handle it. It wasn't as if Newman was giving him a choice and it might work out for the best.

"I'm leaving now," Salazar said, rudely hanging up the phone.

★★★

The archeologists waited in a Giza hotel room for the rest of the Delta Force team to arrive. They hadn't learned anything more than they'd already been told back at the Embassy, so they speculated on the possibilities. They were both still wearing yesterday's rumpled clothes and Mark was getting hungry.

Nuri asked, "Why do you think they chose us to be on this team? Surely they have experts in the government who can advise them on probable terrorist targets in Egypt. What do we know about such things?"

"Nothing," Mark agreed. "I'm guessing they've already recovered some stolen antiquities and we're here to identify what's real or valuable and what's not. The terrorism threat was probably exaggerated to get our cooperation."

"Examining stolen artifacts doesn't make sense," argued Nuri. "They already have people on their payroll to do that. We need to focus on what is unique about you and me that other Egyptologists don't have to offer."

"Several things come to mind, but most of them do not make us desirable." Mark went on to catalogue them. "The Egyptian government doesn't employ us directly because we don't support their premise that the pyramids and other ancient structures were built with slave labor only a few thousand years ago. We both earned our doctorates at Harvard rather than Cairo University. Our work here is barely tolerated by the Egyptian government, for political reasons. Neither of us has a chance of getting permits to excavate significant sites in Egypt, as long as we are out of favor with the reigning archeological authorities here. Those facts don't make us very popular. If we were really their first choice, it had to be for other reasons."

Nuri sighed, "When you put it like that, this whole story being a big hoax still sounds plausible. Nothing else makes sense. But why would they want to humiliate us?"

Mark suddenly got a scared look on his face. "Maybe this thing really is dangerous and they picked us because the risk of being hurt or killed is so high. They aren't looking for quality Egyptologists; they're looking for expendable experts."

Nuri finally realized they had let their imaginations run wild. "Let's wait until the others get here to discuss this any further. We're jumping to conclusions that probably aren't true. It sounds like you think the Director or General, or whatever he is, was lying to us. What I heard him say was that they are taking our safety quite seriously."

They each stared off into the distance for almost a minute. Now they were both a little embarrassed they had jumped to such far-fetched conclusions based only on assumptions. Without another word, Mark picked up the room service menu as Nuri switched on his laptop.

Chapter 23

A special tone on his computer told Mansur an urgent email had just arrived. It was from Amir, saying the plan had been severely compromised. He said the Americans knew everything except that the Suez Canal was being targeted. The warehouse was under constant surveillance and his people would be arrested the moment they drove away from the building with the Cubane. This warning made Mansur smile.

He responded that all was well because he had already transported the Cubane to another location. Mansur doubted that even Ramin was aware of this. The agents who followed them from the Cubane test site thought their surveillance of the warehouse had gone unnoticed. Mansur had planned ahead by obtaining duplicates of the suitcases that contained the Cubane. Using some sleight of hand in the loading, the Hummer ended up with the empty suitcases while those holding the Cubane had been spirited out of the warehouse in a nondescript passenger car. They didn't know it, but the Mossad agents had been keeping a close watch on harmless luggage. However, Mansur did have a different sort of 'bombshell' loaded inside the Hummer. It would be quite a surprise for both Ramin and the Americans.

★★★

Mansur was waiting for two of his men to bring him the luggage containing the Cubane. He had to remain hidden until the team left for Suez because the Americans might know his face. He cursed Sadad for allowing the infidels to get their hands on that laptop. The security precautions he'd installed on the computer probably erased all the damaging data, but he was taking no chances.

As he waited, Mansur carefully reviewed the details of the mission and his team. Some of the members were handpicked from the soldiers of Mohammed's Faithful. Every one of those men had already proven themselves in battle. He recruited others from Afghanistan because it was important that the people he didn't know would want to return home immediately after the mission was completed. The farther away their homes were from Egypt, the better. They were all highly trained and he was certain he could count on them, especially at the prices Amir paid.

An entire upper floor in a luxury condo complex in New Cairo had been rented by Amir to house the team. There was an impressive small scale model of the target locations along the Suez Canal to clearly diagram everyone's assignment. The five locations were to be destroyed at the same time, even though they were spread out over the entire length of the canal. The Israeli detonators could be coded to accept the same encrypted satellite frequency making this simultaneous detonation possible from anywhere in the world.

The location of his men and the Cubane were unknown to the authorities, so they were already past the riskiest phase of the mission. Hijacking the Suez train, setting the charges and blowing up the targets would be easy compared to all they had done to get to this point. Still, he'd feel better once his men delivered the Cubane to his hotel room. The final phase of the mission would begin with the setting of the sun.

★★★

Bashir and Kazim had been responsible for getting the luggage out of the warehouse and delivered to Mansur's hotel room in Giza. They were excited to play such a key role in one of the largest freedom fighting operations in history. Now that Mansur had the suitcases, their orders were to drive around Cairo until it was time to meet the team back at the hotel. As Bashir drove away from the hotel, they started talking about the money and notoriety this job would bring them.

Their success would be revered throughout their shrouded world of mercenaries. That meant, in the future, they would be paid higher wages. Perhaps they would be chosen to lead future missions. They enjoyed the idea of giving the orders instead of always taking them. This made both men reflect on whether or not they were ready for such responsibility. "What makes Mansur a good leader?" Kazim asked.

"We're smart. We are also fearless and will stop at nothing until we accomplish what we set out to do. Didn't we deliver the suitcases just as Mansur wanted?" Bashir said with a defiant lift to his chin. "It all comes down to one thing. If we too had some of that powerful explosive, we would be his competition instead of his employees."

"Perhaps you are right. I heard about the huge explosion when they tested it. That blast came from a little ball that could fit in your fist." Kazim cupped his hand to illustrate his point. Both men were thinking the same thing but it was Kazim who said it out loud.

"What if we remove some of the Cubane from a suitcase before we take it from the hotel to the vehicles? There is so much, surely no one would miss it."

Bashir thought for a moment and said, "We wouldn't want to carry it around with us. We must store it somewhere until we can come back for it later."

"We don't need much," Kazim added. "Perhaps the same amount as the ball they tested back at the warehouse?"

Bashir added, "We might as well each take some, if we take any at all. There is enough to destroy all the targets twice over. But how would we get it out of the hotel? We should have thought of this before we delivered the suitcases. Mansur will see everything we do, once we leave the hotel for Suez."

"Then we hide it inside the hotel and come back for it. I already know how we can do this. We drop the Cubane down the laundry chute and ask your brother Nantu to pick it up. He lives nearby in Cairo, doesn't he?" Kazim asked Bashir.

"Yes, but I don't know if he would do this for us. He deals only in drugs, not weapons."

"It wouldn't hurt to ask him. He doesn't have to know what it is exactly. Tell him the balls are drugs mixed in with clay to disguise them. Tell Nantu you agreed to deliver the drugs before you committed to this better-paying job. Tell him you'll split the delivery money with him, if he'll help."

Bashir had to admit that the plan would probably work. He pulled out his cell phone and called Nantu. His brother knew of the hotel, and had done business there on occasion. He agreed to go collect the "drugs" whenever Bashir called to say they had been left in the basement near or under the laundry chute.

★★★

Captain Paul Saunders had been put in charge of the special Delta Force team tasked with stopping the terrorist plot in Egypt. Saunders wasn't given much to go on. He knew that a group armed with unstable Cubane explosives was planning to destroy one or more high-value targets in Cairo or Alexandria. Their intel was that these were mercenary soldiers rather than religious zealots. That was good because mercenaries were driven by profit rather than wanting to die for Allah. That would make it a lot easier for Saunders' men to take them alive and avoid a huge fireworks show in the process.

Mossad operatives were keeping the warehouse under constant surveillance and stood ready to call Saunders, the moment the Cubane was moved. In the meantime, Saunders' people were staked out along the nearby highway, ready to box the terrorists in, once they turned onto the main road.

From the moment Saunders' people had deployed in Cairo, he had been keeping Washington in the loop on the mission's latest developments, and vice versa. It was a welcomed surprise when the identity of the terrorist leader was confirmed. Colonel Achmed Mansur's picture pulled from the laptop video in Israel had been positively matched to the pictures taken by the Mossad agents at the site of the test explosion in Egypt.

Additional intel, recovered from the laptop by the CIA techs, tied Mansur's actions directly to the Syrian government. There was definitive proof that Mansur had led military assaults against U.S. soldiers that deployed biological weapons, as well as destroying the supply depot in Israel. Saunders knew Mansur had to be stopped, even if it cost he and his men their lives. They all knew that outcome was possible when they signed on for this mission. Remembering that the alternative was an all-out war in the Middle East made the choice easier.

★★★

Saunders thought the following update from Washington had to be a mistake. He was told that two archeologists had been added to his Delta Force team. No further explanation came with the order. He called the phone number he was given to make contact with them, hoping to confirm this was a misunderstanding. Unfortunately, Mark and Nuri asked the same question he was about to ask them. "What need is there for two archeologists on this mission?" Paul sighed and told them his orders were to keep them both safe and on standby during the operation. To Mark and Nuri's great disappointment, that was the end of their briefing. They would have to console themselves with unlimited room service and a gorgeous fifteenth floor view of the Giza pyramids.

Saunders had no choice but to assign two of his men to go to the civilians' hotel room and stay with them at all times. An emergency response vehicle was also assigned to them in case the archeologists were actually needed.

★★★

Saunders and the rest of his men were growing impatient waiting east of New Cairo for the Mossad agents to call. The plan was to have a local Egyptian police car, with Saunders' men inside, pull the Hummer over. If the suspected terrorists made a run for it, the four vehicles led by Saunders would intercept them. If they did pull over, Saunders' men in the police car would detain the Hummer until the Humvees arrived and surrounded the vehicle. Nothing fancy, but the plan should be effective.

The problem was that the Hummer was still sitting in the warehouse, unattended. Egyptian troops had already set up a wide roadblock perimeter to ensure no traffic was allowed on the section of road where Saunders and his men were waiting. The longer they waited in the afternoon sun, the more anxious they became. They didn't know the oncoming darkness meant the waiting would soon be over.

Chapter 24

Finally, Saunders got the call from the Mossad agent that the Hummer had left the warehouse and had turned west toward New Cairo. Saunders knew their super-charged Humvees could outrun and surround the glossy black civilian Hummer. What he didn't know, was if the terrorists, with all that unstable Cubane, would choose to live or kill them all.

Saunders's people were still about five kilometers in front of the team in the Egyptian police car when they notified him that they were ready to pull the suspects over. He gave them the go-ahead and warned the men in his convoy to stay alert.

The soldiers in the police cruiser turned on their flashing lights and, to everyone's surprise, the Hummer pulled over immediately. The headlights of the oncoming Humvees could be seen in the distance as the Hummer and police car stopped along the gravel shoulder of the highway. The police cruiser's team leader radioed that they were stopped behind the suspect's vehicle. Saunders responded that his convoy was still a minute out when the Hummer started rolling backwards.

Suddenly, the Hummer's gear shift was slammed into reverse as the driver punched the accelerator pedal to the floor. The vehicle's tires spit gravel everywhere as the monstrous SUV lunged backward toward the police cruiser. The team braced for the impact that would set off the unstable Cubane.

The collision jolted the police car, pushing it backward several yards, but nothing exploded. They were shocked to still be alive. The Hummer's driver immediately jammed the gearshift into drive and the suspects fishtailed their way back onto the highway. The soldiers tried to pursue the suspects but the police car wouldn't budge. It was immobilized, with the left fender gouged deep into the front tire. The team leader radioed their status to Captain Saunders and warned that the Hummer was headed his way at full speed.

★★★

Saunders was amazed that the collision and unstable Cubane hadn't killed them all. He ordered his team's drivers to execute a quick U-turn. Their plan required that the Humvees travel in the same direction as the Hummer to be able to safely box in the suspects. He hoped their luck would hold in getting the Hummer to stop without casualties.

He radioed to the Egyptian roadblock to prepare for the worst. The suspect vehicle had to be stopped prior to reaching the barricade! The lives of many innocent people were hanging on Saunders' ability to end this chase now, one way or another.

The shiny black Hummer flew past the Humvees at more than 130 kph. Three of the team's vehicles let it go by knowing the Captain's Humvee was still a distance ahead of them. As the speeding Hummer approached, Saunders' driver began to match its movements so that it couldn't pass. The other three Humvees caught up doing more than 175 kph as they deployed in a U formation. With Saunders' vehicle still in front, they surrounded the Hummer, matching its speed, to cut off any chance of escape.

The men in the Hummer began to panic when they realized what was happening, but it was too late! They tried to force their way out of the moving box by swerving left and then right, but they were too close to the Humvees to break free. The scene looked like a game of close-quarters bumper cars as all four Humvees kept shoving the Hummer back into a tight formation as they continued to slow.

When all five vehicles were stopped in the middle of the deserted highway, soldiers emerged from the Humvees and aimed their weapons at the mysterious vehicle's darkened windows. In both Arabic and English the suspects were told to crawl out of the side windows of the vehicle with their hands exposed and empty. Everyone tensed as the windows were rolled down. Empty hands were shown first and the occupants of the vehicle did as they were ordered.

There were only two men inside the Hummer. Soon they were lying face-down on the road with a combat boot on each of their backs as they were handcuffed. Other soldiers quickly searched the vehicle. When they discovered that the decoy suitcases were empty, Saunders realized they'd been had.

An interrogation of the two men did not reveal the location of the Cubane, but it did explain why the men had bolted. At first, they claimed they had run because they thought they were being hijacked. Then they surprised everyone by confessing that they had been hired to dispose of a dead body that was hidden under the steel cargo plate in the rear of the Hummer. Wrapped in plastic sheeting and duct tape was the decomposing body of a woman in western clothing. She was quickly identified as Karen Moffitt, the missing Assistant to the First Lady.

A very pissed-off Captain Saunders realized this entire scenario had been choreographed to distract them from the actual mission. He had to inform his command center that the terrorists were still at large with the Cubane. Worse yet, he had no idea where they were or how to track them down.

★★★

Mansur was pleased his men had arrived at his hotel room in staggered order to avoid attention. Kazim and Bashir were the last to arrive. The Colonel took the lead and guided the group to the stairwell leading to the parking lot where their cars were waiting. There was plenty of time to load the small suitcases into their vehicles and convoy to the south end of the Suez Canal. He took a moment to congratulate himself on getting to this point. Commandeering the train before sunrise would be easy because most of the operators were unarmed. Setting the Cubane charges at the five strategic points along the canal would be easier still. Then Mansur would make history with the push of a button. He smiled knowing the American's peace plan was doomed.

As the men filed out of the stairwell, the Colonel received the text he'd been waiting for. It said that the Americans had chased down the Hummer on the highway east of New Cairo. Mansur was amused because there was no evidence that tied him to the kidnapping of the First Lady or the woman's death. Ramin was their only suspect so his death would tie up any loose ends. Mansur was confident that he would eliminate Ramin before the authorities could question him.

★★★

Kazim and Bashir made sure they were the last to leave the hotel room. The moment they were alone, Kazim opened the suitcase and scooped up as much Cubane as his hands could hold. He formed that into a ball about twelve centimeters across. Bashir said nothing, but took only enough of the substance to make a small sphere about a third the size of the first. After he smoothed over the holes they had just created, Bashir closed the suitcase and pocketed the ball. Kazim was already headed for the laundry chute at the west end of the hallway. Bashir raced out into the hall knowing they had to move quickly to avoid Mansur's suspicion.

As Kazim reached the laundry chute, he slid the door open. Bashir watched as his friend tossed the softball sized sphere into the opening. He motioned quickly to Bashir to hurry, when the unstable Cubane ball hit the basement floor 30 meters below.

The explosion that shook the bowels of the building sent an incredible fireball up through the laundry chute. It blasted like a flamethrower into the seventh floor hallway. Bashir watched in horror as his friend's upper body virtually disintegrated from the intense heat. A tremendous quake rose up from the building's foundation as the west end of the old hotel began to collapse.

Bashir spun away from the blast hoping to escape down the east stairwell. Time seemed to stop when he felt something strike his head. A broken brick from the explosion hit the side of his face with such force that he heard his own neck snap. He still hadn't understood what had happened when he involuntarily dropped to his knees. He was trying to feel where the brick had hit him, but his arm wouldn't respond. He was dead the next moment. The suitcase of Cubane was lying next to his body ready to finish off what was left of the building.

★★★

Colonel Mansur wasn't sure if he instinctively hit the ground or was thrown there, when the explosion erupted. He couldn't see the massive damage to the west side of the hotel, from where he stood in the parking lot. He correctly guessed that some small amount of the Cubane had been detonated by accident, though he couldn't imagine how. He had the detonators with him. A quick count of the men on the ground told him two still remained inside. That meant a suitcase full of Cubane was also inside and at risk of exploding as well.

Mansur managed to get to his feet and ran back to the stairwell. He climbed the steps quickly, but he could see that the building was beyond repair. He could hear the other hotel guests screaming and calling for help. When he arrived at the seventh floor, he had to force open the door to access the hallway. He was vexed to see that, through the thick smoke, the far end of the corridor was open to the night sky. He saw a man lying face down about five meters in front of him with a suitcase by his side. Mansur moved forward cautiously because it sounded and felt like the building was ready to collapse at any moment. When he reached the body, he could barely tell it was Bashir, due to the severe gash to his face.

Mansur knew he had to get the suitcase safely out of the hotel, but he had another problem. If Bashir and Kazim were identified too quickly, that information could lead the police to the entire team. A quick search of the dead man's pockets yielded his wallet and a ball of clay that Mansur immediately recognized as Cubane. The fool was trying to steal some for his own use! That partially explained the explosion and let him know not to bother looking for Kazim. He would count the detonators later to see if any were missing.

He pocketed the wallet as he picked up the suitcase and headed back to the stairwell. If he was lucky, they would still be able to get the team under way before the first responders arrived on the scene. When he reached the ground floor and went outside, he found his men searching for him. Apparently no one had seen him reenter the hotel's stairwell. They were relieved he was unharmed and that the mission was still a go. Mansur yelled that they needed to leave immediately as he handed the suitcase with the Cubane off to Shallal, his Second in Command. They all went to their cars and turned on their radios to hear Mansur's instructions.

Police cars and fire trucks had just begun to arrive on the scene and they blocked the driveways and streets surrounding the hotel. Mansur cursed that he had opted to go with civilian cars to keep a low profile. Anything with four-wheel-drive would have made it easy to escape. Regardless, they had to leave now or abandon the vehicles. He looked around for any exits from the property. He radioed for everyone to follow him, then he slowly drove up a curb and over a landscape berm toward a possible exit. He had passed the point of turning back when he discovered his chosen route was blocked by a fire truck.

Mansur jumped out of his sedan to move the vehicle out of the way. As he had hoped, the engine was running. He jumped up into the cab and put it in gear. He had only moved a few meters when two firemen ran to the driver's door and began yelling at him. Mansur ignored them until they opened the door and tried to forcibly pull him out. He cursed their stupidity, as he shot them both. He had no quarrel with these men, but they had left him no choice.

Mansur finished moving the firetruck so that it was not only out of the way but it hid the bodies of the two firemen as well. When he made it back to his vehicle, he saw the situation had gone from bad to worse! His men had all driven in different directions, trying to find another exit. He radioed to them that they were on their own to get off the hotel property. He ordered them to meet at the backup rendezvous point in an hour and to make certain they weren't followed. With that, he slowly forced his car past the firetruck, traffic and the gawking people.

Chapter 25

Captain Saunders was hoping for a break. He felt responsible for losing track of the Cubane and failing to identify more of the terrorists or their target. He was certain that there would be an event to rival 9/11 in the next 24 hours, if they didn't catch up with these bastards.

His break arrived a moment later when the command post informed him there had been a huge explosion at a hotel in Giza. There were no other details available but Saunders knew this had to be Mansur's doing. He contacted the rest of his team by radio to head to Giza. Hopefully he'd have more information by the time they arrived.

★★★

As their convoy of Humvees approached Giza, Saunders could see the bright work lights contrasting against the smoke and ash of the crumbling hotel. He wondered how much of the Cubane had detonated. Certainly not much if only this one building was damaged. But why would they detonate only a tiny portion of what they had? Was this another ruse to throw them off?

The only face Saunders knew for sure was Mansur's and that was from the facial recognition photos Mossad and the CIA had provided. He tried to figure out how Mansur would be traveling. Was he using a large team with several vehicles or was it just one dangerously loaded truck? Were they after one target or many? Would Mansur be going for the maximum loss of life, maximum financial damage, or perhaps targets that would elicit the greatest emotional impact? He assumed a man like that wouldn't settle for less than achieving all three.

★★★

Egypt's evening news was reporting the hotel explosion at the same time George Salazar's flight arrived in Cairo. As the jet approached the airport runway, he could see the flashing lights in the distance from dozens of emergency vehicles blurred by the continuous smoke and ash from the charred remains of the hotel. He guessed that Mansur's thugs were behind the commotion and he wondered if hitting the Suez Canal was still possible after drawing that much attention.

Once inside the airport terminal, he called Mansur from a payphone. He didn't want the call to be traced back to him if Mansur had already been apprehended. The Colonel picked up after the sixth ring and Salazar immediately took on the persona of Amir.

"You couldn't wait to get started or is this all part of your great plan?" Amir began sarcastically. "The last time we spoke you said you had everything under control."

"The mission is still on but there have been complications," Mansur calmly admitted.

"I'm calling from a payphone in Cairo, so I'll get the details later. Under the circumstances, I think we need to meet. Where would you suggest?" Amir added.

"Are you familiar with our staging area outside of Suez?" Mansur asked.

"The abandoned building just beyond the city limits?"

"Yes. Meet me there an hour before sunrise. Bring Ramin for I have much to tell both of you. If I am late, I will not be coming and the operation is aborted."

Mansur hung up and calculated how he would get to the backup rendezvous point in Giza without being identified. He wanted to skirt the city and stay off the main roads but he also needed to be on the southwest side of Giza in fifteen minutes. There was no way around it. He would have to get on the Al Ahram highway to arrive on time.

★★★

Captain Saunders split his men into three groups to be on the lookout for Mansur and his mercenaries, however many there were. His best guess was that Mansur was planning to detonate the Cubane at the Cairo Museum or the Great Pyramid of Giza, or both. He ordered his people to patrol those locations in hopes of spotting any suspicious activity.

The two locations were approximately ten kilometers apart to the east and west of each other. Saunders left his driver with the museum team and decided to drive himself back and forth between the two stakeout locations. The more eyes they had everywhere looking for Mansur, the better the odds were of catching him. The streets were oddly void of traffic. The locals in this part of the world knew better than to go sight-seeing once trouble started.

In the meantime, a search of the warehouse in New Cairo revealed it contained some serious weaponry but no Cubane. None of the people left behind in the warehouse, nor the two men from the Hummer, had any idea what was going on. It became clear they were hired in the past few days and were set up to take the fall for Ramin and Mansur.

Saunders tried to anticipate Mansur's next move. He figured the hotel explosion was a mistake rather than part of his plan. He heard that two of the fire fighters had been shot by a man who tried to steal a firetruck parked outside the hotel. The description was vague but it could have been Mansur himself. That would indicate the Cubane detonation was as much a surprise to him as it was for the citizens of Giza. From the description Saunders was given about the damage to the hotel, a small quantity was apparently all that had ignited. That meant if Mansur hadn't known before, he now knew that the Cubane was unstable.

Saunders saw a sedan approaching him on the Al Ahram highway leaving Giza toward the pyramids. The oncoming sedan was the only other vehicle he could see on the empty road. When they were no more than 30 meters apart, he flicked on his bright headlights to get a good view of the person driving toward him. The man automatically raised his hand to block the glare, but Saunders thought he looked like Mansur. He decided to follow that car until he was sure either way.

★★★

Mansur confirmed via radio that his men were already at the backup rendezvous location. He was close to the turn he would take to join them, but then an oncoming car flashed its high beams just as they passed each other. Normally, he would have cursed them and thought nothing about it, but he saw the vehicle turning around in the distance in his rear view mirror. He got back on the radio and told the team leader he had picked up a tail. He instructed Shallal to get the men and their vehicles out of sight. They should wait fifteen minutes so Mansur could lead the other vehicle away from them, then they could proceed to Suez without him. He'd shake the person tailing him and catch up before morning.

★★★

Shallal considered his dilemma. There was only one place to hide their vehicles completely out of sight, without getting on the highway, and that was behind a locked gate. Even if they broke the chains and parked where they could not be seen, he feared they would not remain hidden for long. If Mansur had been spotted driving alone, what chance did their five vehicles have of being unnoticed when the streets were so deserted? After dark, no one visited this area. The site of the Sphinx was a tourist favorite, but the visiting hours ended when the sun went down taking the tourists' picture opportunities with it. Mansur had ordered them to wait 15 minutes, and he knew better than to cross the Colonel.

Shallal cut the chains to the gate blocking the access path that led to the excavation pit surrounding the Sphinx. He ordered everyone to follow him in their vehicles. They went down the compacted dirt ramp that was set against the wall on one side but was open to the pit on the other. It descended at a fairly steep angle and had a ninety-degree right turn after it cleared the front of the limestone statue. The excavated pit surrounding the base of the Sphinx was perhaps 30 meters wide and 10 meters deep separating the limestone pedestal of the statue from the dirt walls.

Once they had all parked, Shallal checked his watch again. Only two minutes had passed. This was going to be the longest 15 minutes of his life. He pulled to the front of the other cars that were now parked in a straight line along the south side of the Sphinx. They were strategically positioned to make a quick exit when it was time.

As they waited, he considered how to keep the lowest profile possible. All of their vehicles had been fitted with a kill switch for their lights when a total blackout was needed. However, there was a problem with turning off all their lights. The inclined dirt road was perhaps a meter wider than the width of a standard car. It had been tough to maneuver the cars down the ramp as it was. Without any lights at all, they would have to move even more slowly as they exited or risk going over the unprotected side into the pit. He looked at his watch again. Not even three minutes had gone by. He got back on the radio and ordered the drivers to kill all their lights until they were back on the highway.

At three and a half minutes, Shallal was so anxious he almost started his car to leave. He strained to hear any traffic noise from the nearby highway. He kept expecting to hear the sirens of many vehicles converging upon them. He panicked realizing this pit was only a good hiding place if no one was looking for them, and that was hardly the case.

At three minutes and forty-seven seconds, Shallal was done waiting. He told everyone to start their vehicles and to follow his lead. He put the gearshift into drive and slowly pulled forward. It was difficult to see if they were all behind him because it was so dark. He continued forward until he could see the beginning of the dirt ramp that would take them out of the pit. He had to trust that the other cars were keeping up with him.

He made the sharp left turn and continued up the narrow ramp when one of the cars behind him flashed his lights, trying to see where to make the turn. Shallal was immediately enraged. Breaking discipline like that would get them all caught or even killed. He angrily turned his head to see who it was as he grabbed his radio to warn the fool against doing that again. That was when his left front tire rolled halfway off the ramp's graded edge.

At first, he didn't notice his wheel had caught because he was still yelling into the radio. He finished his tirade by slapping the radio down on the seat beside him. He then stepped on the gas but found that the steering wheel wouldn't turn. He realized that the tire was about to drop off the left edge. He tried not to panic, as he pulled hard to the right to force the wheel back up on to the ramp. At that same moment, the car behind him bumped his fender. Though their cars hardly touched, it was just enough to crack open the gates of hell.

Shallal felt his left front tire slide off the edge of the ramp. He heard a crunching sound as the left ball joint collapsed under the direct weight of the car. His vehicle was tilting now, as it skidded on its chassis toward the pit some five meters below. In desperation, he jammed the car into reverse and tried to pull the left front wheel back onto the dirt road. At first, it started to back up just the way he wanted. Then his car bumped back into the vehicle behind him and the rear wheels lost traction and began to spin. His car resumed sliding forward along the edge of the dirt ramp. He felt the right-side wheels leave the ground as the car tipped over and began falling toward the bottom of the pit.

He thought he might be able to survive the fall depending on how the car landed. He braced for the impact, but the unstable Cubane was not to be denied.

In the blink of an eye, so many things no longer mattered. Turning on the headlights was not important anymore. Staying hidden wasn't something they'd have to worry about. The Suez Canal mission ceased to be a concern. The blast from Shallal's car set off a chain reaction of the Cubane stashed in the other vehicles. The combined explosions shook the ground as far away as ten kilometers from ground zero. Observers might assume the ominous mushroom cloud was the result of a missile strike but it was simply the largest quantity of Cubane ever detonated in one place at one time.

When the smoke and dust began to clear, what remained of the Sphinx looked more like a lump of stone than the magnificent statue it had been just minutes before. The surrounding pit was now a huge crater. The only remaining sign of Shallal and his team were shiny bits of their cars falling like hail stones mixed with debris from the statue and surrounding earth. For thousands of years, humankind had marveled at the beauty of the Sphinx. In the blink of an eye, it was gone forever.

Chapter 26

The sun was still shining in Washington when President Alexander was told the Sphinx had been destroyed just minutes ago. He barely kept the anger out of his voice to ask if the Cubane had been used. If so, it was a solid connection to Achmed Mansur. There had been no confirmation yet, but the blast was so large that the Cubane had to be the cause.

Matt closed his eyes, hung his head and considered the chances of his peace plan working when this event hit the world news. Realistically, he knew they were zero. His knee-jerk reaction was to prepare the U.S. military for the inevitable violence to follow. He was about to call General McComb when he remembered his promise to Erin. He swore he would not make a decision of this nature for at least 24-hours. Even when he had made that promise, he knew it would be difficult to keep. He hesitated, hung up the phone, and took a moment to reflect.

How could so few people be allowed to disrupt such unprecedented cooperation among nations? He felt an overwhelming loss knowing a lasting peace had been within their grasp. Despite everyone's best efforts toward peace, war was now the more likely outcome. Could life really be this unfair?

In the midst of his despair, Matt flashed on his déjà vu memory of the briefing with the man dressed in white. He had been encouraged to not lose faith in the peace plan when it got to this point. He remembered this latest conflict began to escalate in the fabled place known as Armageddon. He winced at the vision he had of the whole world walking through that valley of death.

Through his mental anguish, a flash of inspiration seemed to burst through his mind. He needed to snap out of it and start doing something useful. His next thought was of the two archeologists he had added to the Delta Force team in pursuit of Mansur. While it made no sense at the time, he now remembered why they needed to be at the site of the Sphinx, or what was left of it. Matt had to hope they had not been injured in all the chaos. He sent out the order that they should be the first responders to inspect the ground zero location before anyone else had a chance. He offered no further explanation knowing the answer would be clear when they arrived.

★★★

Captain Saunders was three kilometers away from the Sphinx when the Cubane detonated. The blinding flash, shaking road and tremendous gale force rush of wind were unbelievable. Within seconds, there was sand and other debris raining down all around him. He lost sight of the vehicle Mansur may have been driving; but that was secondary to his concern for his team patrolling the nearby Great Pyramid. He pulled his car over and looked back at the ominous glow just outside of Giza.

Saunders fumbled around for his radio that had fallen to the floor of the vehicle. He was unable to raise anyone from the team so he tried the command post. They did respond but had no information about the status of the team monitoring the pyramids. His men at the Cairo Museum had asked for instructions after seeing and feeling the blast in the distance. Saunders instructed them to stay alert since the museum might be next.

He then asked the command post to contact Washington and request additional orders now that prevention of this tragedy was no longer an option. They responded with a strange directive from the White House. The orders were to get the two archeologists to the Sphinx site as quickly as possible and let no one else in for as long as they could peacefully keep them out.

Saunders radioed the information to his team members assigned to protect the two civilians. He was told they were already driving in that direction. The four men had felt the foundation of their hotel shake when the Cubane exploded. From the panoramic view their hotel room provided, they could see an eerie mushroom cloud against the night sky. It hovered like an oddly shaped exclamation point somewhere above the Sphinx. Mark and Nuri had practically forced the soldiers to take them there immediately.

Saunders had an idea on how they could fulfill the orders from the White House. He told them to arrive in MOPP – mission oriented protective posture – gear as if the site were contaminated. The Cubane residue did not pose a health hazard but his men would quickly lose control of the detonation zone if the Egyptian first responders were able to seal the place off. If Saunders had his people tell the local authorities that the area was lethally contaminated, no one would go near the blast site without suitable protection. They would prefer to wait until they heard it was all clear or their own protective gear was available. Saunders told the command post to update all team members of this change in their plan.

★★★

Mark and Nuri were heartbroken over the destruction of the Sphinx, but they began to appreciate why they were on this team. The soldier riding in the back of the vehicle with them demonstrated how to put on the MOPP gear. He assured them that there was no radiation threat from the Cubane, but there was no telling what else might have been a part of that explosion. He also told them they wouldn't have long to investigate the scene without interference from the local authorities.

The cloud over the rubble of the Sphinx was already dissipating in the nighttime sky. When they arrived at the perimeter, Saunders' own men waved them through. When the Cubane blew up, they had all been staked out on the far side of the Great Pyramid. That shielded them from the worst of the blast. They were badly shaken up for a time but had no serious injuries among them. They confirmed they would try to hold everyone else back for as long as they could.

The soldier pulled up as close as he could get to the blast site and parked. He quickly donned his MOPP gear and the four men proceeded to ground zero. Inside the crater was a sharply angled lump that had once been the hind end of the Sphinx. The rest had been blown away by the force of the explosion.

They made their way down the side of the crater where the Sphinx had been just minutes before. They were able to make out several odd formations revealed in the crater's walls that had been below ground. Mark and Nuri looked at each other, both realizing what these anomalies in the terrain meant. They weren't just archeologists' tunnels dug out of the dirt; they were actual passageways built to last and constructed of cut boulders for maximum support. Nuri pointed to a large breach in a particular passageway and Mark agreed that was the best place to enter. The stone tunnel led in the direction where the right paw of the Sphinx had once pointed.

One of the soldiers remained at the entrance to keep watch while the other went with Mark and Nuri. With flashlights in hand, they trekked down the sloping tunnel until they came upon a 180-degree turn that headed back toward the Sphinx. The downward incline was fairly steep and it was difficult to judge how deep they were going below the original ground level. It felt to Mark as if the passage went as far back as it did forward, so they were probably now close to being directly under where the right paw of the Sphinx had been.

The significance of this was not lost on either archeologist. They looked at each other and nodded their mutual agreement of what they had discovered. In 1933, the American clairvoyant Edgar Cayce had claimed that some sort of "Hall of Records" existed at this precise spot. According to him, its eventual discovery would prove the existence of an advanced civilization from thousands of years ago. It was Mark and Nuri's open-mindedness that such things once existed that caused the Egyptian government to question their credibility as scientists.

They continued forward through the darkness, the beams from their flashlights bouncing around the walls of the tunnel. The passage turned right and led to a larger room. Just as Cayce had said, the Hall of Records would be found entering from the right paw of the Sphinx into a larger chamber centered beneath the paws. Their excitement grew as they approached an ornately carved door that had buckled and fallen away from the quaking impact of the explosion. They were able to step over the rubble into the room beyond. The soldier followed them into the room but was still watchful of anyone approaching from behind.

Once they were inside the chamber, each man was mesmerized by what it contained. The glow from their flashlights illuminated the entire room. The frescoes on the walls were not the typical profile or side-view depictions of ancient Egyptian rulers and slaves. They were beautiful drawings of a culture, technology and architecture unknown to the archeologists. The murals looked as if they had been painted by Rembrandt for their detail and likeness to real life.

Most notable were the large stone tablets mounted on the walls setting them apart from others that were lying in pieces on the floor of the chamber. A quick count told Mark and Nuri there were 32 of the mounted tablets, eight on each of the four walls. They remembered Edgar Cayce had said much of humanity's ancient history was recorded and stored in three places throughout the world. He had predicted that the most accessible of those locations was the Hall of Records beneath the paws of the Sphinx. The mounted stone tablets contained a great deal of writing and symbols using an alphabet unknown to either scientist. The rest of the room held all manner of strange artifacts that were not identifiable at first glance. Some might have been musical instruments while other objects seemed to consist of complex technology whose purpose was unclear.

Suddenly, the ground started to settle and all three men braced themselves as the quake rattled the room and their nerves. Huge cracks appeared in the walls and it was clear the room was in danger of collapsing. When the noise and shifting finally subsided, they moved quickly knowing they might have to evacuate at any moment.

Nuri produced a camera and started taking still-shot pictures of the wall murals and the 32 tablets. Mark started capturing what he could on video of the strange objects displayed on the ornately decorated shelving that lined the walls below the tablets. The soldier was fixated on eight waist-high shiny black pedestals forming a circle around the center of the room. He approached the one closest to him and saw that it had a polished impression of a hand centered on the top. The soldier placed his right hand on the pedestal so that it matched the imprint and a strange noise filled the chamber.

Nuri and Mark both turned in surprise; their jaws dropped as a bright light filled the room emanating from the ground at the center of the circle of pedestals. As it intensified, a small object separated itself from the stone floor and rose into the air. All eyes were on this new curiosity as it elevated and then hovered about two meters above the floor. The soldier removed his hand from the pedestal but the artifact remained suspended in mid-air. Nuri finally collected himself enough to take more pictures of this amazing scene. Mark realized he had forgotten he was still recording video and aimed his camera toward the center of the chamber.

As Mark approached a different pedestal, he had to switch the camera to his right hand because the impression in the smooth stone was for the left hand only. He could feel a rush of energy pass through his body as he pressed his hand against the polished surface. Then a focused beam of white light from the center of the floor connected with the floating object above it. At first, the intense dust in the air reflected the light so much it was overwhelming. When their eyes adjusted to the brightness, they could see that the beam from the floor had divided into multiple rays of light. Each ray connected a device lying on the shelves to the floating object in the middle of the room.

Suddenly, all the technology in the chamber came to life, each device adding to the spectacle with its own lights and sounds. Mark and Nuri continued capturing everything they could with their cameras. They knew this was the most significant archeological discovery in human history. They also knew they would be forced to leave this wondrous place once the Egyptian first responders arrived.

Mark saw a crystalline box lying on a nearby shelf. He felt compelled to pick it up. As he turned to get a better look at it in the light, he thought he must be hallucinating. He saw a 3-D holographic display before him that covered most of the room. He recognized that the panoramic movie unfolding before him matched the locations shown in the fresco paintings he had just recorded on video. He noticed that the hologram changed as he faced different scenes depicted in the wall murals. The hologram was apparently a demonstration of technologies that defied modern explanation.

He saw the construction of the pyramids was made possible through a device that levitated the huge stones. This ancient culture had also been able to produce unlimited quantities of drinking water by removing all the impurities from the Nile and Red Sea. No less remarkable was a scene that apparently took place in the same room where he was standing. The pedestals were being used for healing and rejuvenation of the infirmed.

Without warning, the room began to shudder. As the floor quaked, two of the tablets hanging on the walls came crashing down. Mark was so startled he dropped the crystal box abruptly ending the holographic documentary as it shattered. Objects fell from the shelves and broke into pieces as they landed. The light from the floating object faded to darkness as the room started to collapse. The soldier shouted that they had to leave and no one argued.

Both scientists powered down their cameras as they stumbled toward the exit. The soldier was right behind them when something caught his eye. The floating object had apparently dropped to the floor the moment the chamber went dark. Somehow it had landed right in front of his flashlight beam so he could plainly see it. The soldier scooped up the object, though it now appeared to be broken into two pieces. He slipped them into his pocket and emerged from the chamber just ahead of its final demise.

All three men ran through the tunnel to escape the horrible sounds that seemed to come closer with each step. When they made the turn at the switchback, they realized how desperate the situation was. The crumbling passageway was catching up to them. They ran full speed staying just ahead of the growing cloud of dust. To the amazement of the soldier waiting above ground, they emerged not far from where they had entered the tunnel. He had been certain they would be lost when the terrain started to collapse below.

He told them the Egyptians now had their own MOPP gear and were ignoring the Delta Force team's warnings to stay clear of the blast area. They were expected to arrive on the scene any minute. The soldier who had been with Mark and Nuri made it clear that they had found something extraordinary and could not risk having the Egyptians confiscate their cameras. The archeologists just nodded their agreement still trying to catch their breath.

The soldier who had remained topside already had a plan. The four of them would have to leave the vehicle behind and find another way out. If they moved to the west on foot toward what used to be the rear of the Sphinx, then they could head north unnoticed to the Al Ahram highway. Their own people would be waiting there to pick them up.

All four started running west as fast as they could manage in the crater. They didn't dare use their flashlights and risk alerting the Egyptian responders to their presence. The archeologists were cradling their cameras in case they fell. They were not about to give up the incredible discoveries their digital memories held.

When they reached the far end of the blast site, they looked back to see many flashlight beams dancing in the distance. The Egyptian soldiers had arrived. Mark, Nuri and the two soldiers managed to scramble up the side of the crater and headed north toward the highway. As promised, the Delta Force team was waiting to take them back to the hotel.

Chapter 27

Colonel Mansur had been able to avoid capture, but at what cost? The newscaster on the radio described the destruction of the Sphinx, leaving no doubt that all his team members were dead. He knew they had been together at the backup rendezvous point just minutes before the annihilation of the Sphinx. Whatever set the Cubane off had ensured a spectacular pyrotechnic display to mark their deaths.

The Suez Canal mission, had it succeeded, would have ensured the retelling of their exploits for many years to come. However, it was possible that destroying a national treasure like the Sphinx would serve Amir's purpose just as well. Sadly, it was due to sloppy work. That meant there was no honor in what they had done even if the accidental explosion accomplished the intended goal.

It was then that Mansur remembered that he still had the detonators and the evidence he was supposed to plant at the scene of the explosions. All the other vehicles carried the suitcases packed with Cubane, but he carried the metal shards with the fingerprints of Mossad agents. Unless those prints were found at the scene, nothing would tie Israel to the destruction of the Sphinx. With no known motive or other suspects to distract the investigators, Mansur knew the evidence could lead back to him. That was ironic since the hotel explosion in Giza and demolishing of the Sphinx had been completely unplanned.

What caused the Cubane to explode? He had counted the number of detonators he still held and none were missing. It was so stable a compound that you could hit it with a hammer or shoot it with a bullet and it would have no effect. But what if it was not stable? Maybe it wasn't even Cubane? What if it was a defective batch? That would answer why a cowardly fatah—an Arabic insult—like Ramin would have access to such a rare and expensive substance. The Americans or Israelis probably sold it to him hoping he'd blow himself up the first day.

Perhaps Amir's plan all along was for this debacle to happen. Had Amir colluded with Ramin to procure the defective Cubane from the start? They both knew his explosives expert would handle it carefully in the testing, as a professional would. However, it would most certainly detonate during the mission when rough handling couldn't be avoided. Amir had probably hoped they would all die in the effort and leave no witnesses behind. Even a failed attempt to disrupt passage and commerce through the Suez Canal would stop any efforts toward peace.

What Amir hadn't counted on was Mansur surviving the death of his team. The rest of the world would assume their leader died with them. If there were no surviving witnesses, Mansur could easily change identities and start a new life.

There were only two people left who knew he was still alive. Once they were gone, Mansur would be free to assume a new identity. Amir deserved to die for many reasons. That left Ramin Acaba. He would enjoy killing that coward and tying up the last of the loose ends. He must eliminate both men, alone and without a trace, if the world was to believe that Achmed Mansur had died with his team.

★★★

George Salazar hung up the phone after Langley brought him up to date on the situation in Giza. He had rented a car in Cairo and had already driven to a hotel in Suez. It was near the railway station where the trains went to Port Said at the north end of the canal. He still had a few hours to kill before he met with Mansur outside the city limits.

He had to wonder if Mansur was still alive after the fiasco that destroyed the Sphinx. If he had survived, did he still have a team of mercenaries, let alone any of the Cubane, to attempt the original mission to take out the Suez Canal? He realized that the obliteration of the Sphinx could work just as well to disrupt the peace process, so he finally allowed himself to relax.

The only unresolved detail was the evidence that would implicate the Israelis as the perpetrators who destroyed Egypt's national treasure. Since the incident at the Sphinx was not part of the plan, had Mansur managed to plant the Mossad agents' fingerprints?

A tone from his computer told Salazar that Amir had just received an email. It was a coded message from Mansur saying only that he would make their prearranged meeting at the staging area location as agreed. So he had indeed survived!

It was convenient that "Amir" was already in Egypt because there were loose ends he had to tie up here. Mossad would track down Ramin and force him to reveal the existence of Amir. If they learned Mansur was still alive, they would find and interrogate him. Either way, Amir's presence would be known and that could potentially lead back to him. How long would it take before someone put together that CIA Director George Salazar and the mysterious Amir were the same person? He knew both Ramin and Mansur had to die.

Amir placed a call to Ramin and told him that Mansur planned to kill them both. He invited Ramin to come with him to the pre-dawn meeting with Mansur outside of Suez. He told Ramin to come armed. Amir would make sure Mansur was so distracted by anger that Ramin could easily shoot him. The plan was simple but Achmed Mansur was a trained killer, and neither Amir nor Ramin were in his league when it came to assassinations. They needed this two-to-one advantage to succeed.

★★★

Ramin was certain that both Amir and Mansur would try to kill him if he ever gave them the chance. When Amir called to suggest that they work together to kill Mansur, Ramin reluctantly agreed. Mansur and Amir had to die if he wanted to live through this night. He knew he could not kill them both on his own.

Ramin had been lying low in Suez with several of the mercenaries he worked with regularly. One of them, Abel, was part of the expert sniper team that helped breach and destroy the American supply depot in Israel under Mansur's command. Ramin calculated his best chance to survive this night was to hire Abel to eliminate Mansur and Amir. He considered that Abel might not accept the job if he was hesitant to kill Mansur. He decided that Abel would only see Amir and Mansur in the moonlight as two unidentified men he was being paid to kill. Ramin would not tell him who the targets were and Abel probably wouldn't ask.

When Ramin approached him, Abel quickly agreed to do the job, especially at the fee that was offered. The assignment was straightforward and Abel would have almost no personal risk. A lot of variables could go wrong for Ramin, but that was the nature of the setup. Abel's only condition was that he be paid in advance in case the job was compromised. Ramin had no choice but to trust him given the limited time and circumstances.

Abel left immediately to arrive before anyone else and get set up out of sight of their meeting place. The plan was that Ramin would ride with Amir and wait for Mansur in the parking lot of the abandoned building. Ramin would be sure to stand where he was not in the way of Abel's sight line to the other two. Once they were dead, Ramin and Abel would have the bodies cremated so they would never be identified.

Chapter 28

Ramin pulled into the parking lot with Amir sitting beside him in the passenger seat. They both relaxed a little when they saw no sign of Mansur. That would give them the chance to get set before he arrived, assuming he'd be there. If he didn't show, then Amir planned to take out Ramin and deal with Mansur later.

Amir had a nine millimeter automatic at his side and a snub nose .38 caliber strapped to his ankle. He was also wearing a Kevlar vest. They got out of the car and Amir walked to the spot where he wanted to confront Mansur. Ramin made sure he stood out of the sniper's line of fire as they waited for Mansur to join them.

Amir said, "You really need to calm down. Mansur will know something is wrong if he sees you like this. Are you sure your pistol is in good working order?"

Ramin nervously nodded his head. His voice shook as he said, "I am a businessman, not an assassin. As it is, I have the CIA, Mossad, and probably every Egyptian law enforcement officer looking for me. After this night, I will have to disappear and not come back, ever."

Amir answered, "That is probably for the best. With Mansur eliminated, you will have a much better chance of evading capture. The world will want his head and there will be no one left alive to point an accusing finger at us. They will continue to search for Mansur until his body is found. We must make sure that never happens."

A car turned off the highway and headed toward them. There was no doubt that Mansur was alive and well and was coming to kill them. Amir reminded Ramin to wait until Mansur was angry and distracted before making a move to shoot him. If Mansur wasn't distracted, he would kill them both in a shootout. Ramin nodded, wiped his sweaty hands on his pants, and tried to look calm as the intimidating man walked over to join them.

★★★

Mansur quickly sized up the situation as he parked his car. His brain was hard-wired to calculate his opponents' strengths and weaknesses, especially when walking into an obvious ambush. It was still very dark but he was certain there was someone in the abandoned building approximately fifteen meters away with a rifle aimed in his direction. The two men in front of him would be armed as well but he could easily deal with them.

By their positioning, Mansur could assume that the sniper worked for Ramin. That made sense knowing what a coward he was. He stood facing the building so the sniper would have clear shots at both Amir and Mansur. That meant Amir would probably shoot Ramin at the same moment that Ramin was planning to kill Mansur. It was no secret to him that each man had come to this meeting with the intention of being the only one who walked away. He liked his chances over theirs, but he would have to stay sharp to live beyond the next few minutes.

He planned to keep walking until Amir obstructed his direct line of sight to the old building where the sniper had to be positioned. The sniper would have to kill Amir first to have a clear shot at Mansur. That meant Mansur would shoot Ramin and drop to the ground. Then it would be just him against the hidden gunman. Mansur's ball of Cubane versus the sniper's rifle would be an interesting contest. He was wearing a Kevlar vest and he planned to use the dead men's bodies as additional cover from the Cubane explosion. He knew his plan was dangerous. He was sure to be wounded even if everything went well. However, if Allah willed it, his injuries would not be fatal.

Mansur approached them with both hands in his jacket pockets. He was ambidextrous shooting a pistol, but he could only throw right handed with confidence. The Cubane was in his right pocket and the pistol hidden in his left.

"Good evening my friends!" Mansur began. His smile didn't reach his eyes.

Amir interrupted, "Don't call me friend you incompetent ibn haram (Arabic for bastard). Surmayye a'raasac!" (another terrible Arabic insult). Ramin blinked in surprise but then remembered it was Amir's intention to infuriate Mansur. His excellent choice of insults would likely accomplish this better than Amir had planned.

Mansur started to respond but Amir cut him off again, "Aneekik o aneek ummk o obook o ahlk klhm!" Amir had just threatened Mansur's entire family with rape.

Mansur, still appearing calm, was done talking. Without bothering to pull the pistol from his pocket, he fired twice into Amir's face. He had detected the Kevlar vest beneath Amir's clothing so head shots were the only way to put him down for good. Ramin awkwardly pulled his own gun out and fired but Mansur dodged the shot by dropping to the ground. As he fell, he fired twice at Ramin putting a round in his heart and one that burst into a ghastly crimson spray out the back of his head. Mansur immediately propped up Amir's body to use as protection against the sniper.

Abel opened fire immediately but Mansur had moved fast enough that Amir's vest and body were already protecting him. He could feel the corpse react with every round the sniper fired. Holding the body on its side allowed Mansur to remain concealed as he removed the ball of Cubane from his right pocket. He would have to throw it as hard as he could to ensure it would explode when it hit the building.

Suddenly, a tremendous flash of hot pain shot up Mansur's leg. Abel had figured out the Kevlar vest problem and was now firing at Amir's legs. He knew the bullets would rip through and find his hidden target. Mansur was hit a second time in the right calf and then a third time in the left thigh.

As he readied himself to hurl the Cubane ball, Abel saw that he had a clear shot at Mansur's arm. He pulled the trigger at the same moment Mansur started to throw. Abel's timing was perfect and his round hit Mansur in the wrist. Bones shattered and the sharp impact caused the chunk of Cubane to detonate before it left his hand. It erupted with an explosive force more like an eight-inch artillery shell than a simple hand grenade.

Abel managed to duck for cover but the walls of the dilapidated building disintegrated from the force of the blast. Like oddly shaped jagged cannon balls, the flying bricks and plaster destroyed everything in their path. Abel was mercifully knocked out and somehow survived the devastation. He did not regain consciousness for perhaps twenty minutes. When he did awaken, he was mostly buried under the debris. He had second degree burns everywhere. His left arm was broken above the elbow and he guessed he had a concussion from his massive headache and swollen eyes. There was nothing left around him but rubble and the burnt out shells of their cars. His own car, parked so that it was hidden behind the building, was also totaled.

Abel was certain that Allah wanted these men completely erased, for what else could have caused such an explosion? Surely it was like the end of the world had rained down upon them all. Abel was thankful that he survived, but now he would have to find his way out of this mess. If he could walk to Suez, he had the money to make it the rest of the way home.

Chapter 29

—Three Months Later—

Dr. Mark Heston and Dr. Nuri Zayd wanted everything to be perfect when their VIP visitor came to see the progress they'd made. They were formally trained in archeology, but because of their phenomenal discovery underneath the Sphinx, they had remained an integral part of the team here at Jet Propulsion Laboratory - JPL. It was their skill in translating the text from the 32 tablets that led other scientists to discover the secret of near perpetual energy. The breakthrough would not have succeeded at all if the soldier hadn't stopped to recover the pieces of the floating object just as the chamber collapsed. They were in fact unique crystals designed to tap into the earth's stored power.

The phone rang and Nuri answered it. He hung up and excitedly told Mark, "He's here and on the way up."

A minute later President Alexander walked through the door to the lab with an entourage of scientists and Secret Service agents. This was the first time Mark and Nuri had met the President, although they knew he had personally recommended them to be part of the American team that discovered the Hall of Records beneath the Sphinx.

Matt shook both their hands saying, "Gentlemen, if your reports are accurate, there may never be a more important scientific discovery in the history of humankind than what you have done here in just three months."

"Thank you Mr. President," they both responded. "Please take a seat. We appreciate that your time is limited," said Mark.

The chairs were arranged in a circle around a polished obsidian pedestal and two empty tables in the center of the lab. Eyeglasses with darkly tinted lenses were distributed to everyone in the room. On top of the pedestal were two tetrahedron-shaped crystals twinkling like brilliant diamonds. Unlike the four-sided Great Pyramid of Giza, these were three-sided crystal pyramids roughly the size of a baseball. Mark picked them up and handed them to the President to examine.

"Are these the originals you found under the Sphinx?" Matt asked.

"No sir," Mark answered. "We have found a method to manufacture these perfected crystals from the writings on the tablets that were in that same room. At the moment, they are just pretty rocks. There is no visible difference between them unless they are fused together. When they come together, these two crystals become a conduit for seemingly infinite energy."

Matt tried to push the crystals together trying different combinations and angles. He had read about this unusual development in the initial reports. They remained separate and solid. Mark held out his hands and Matt returned them. Then Mark asked everyone to take their seats as he walked to the pedestal and mounted the crystals on their sides. Their bases were positioned to the outside so each pyramid's topmost point was directly aimed at the other. From his perspective, Matt could see that the triangular bases of the two crystals were offset from each other to form what would look like a six-pointed star. Then Mark nodded at Nuri to throw the switch. A low hum filled the lab. Mark flipped another switch on the pedestal and the crystal points slowly started to move toward each other.

Nuri increased the volume and the low hum became a clearly audible musical note, complete with harmonic tones. The sound was almost human for it seemed to be pronouncing the syllable "oh." The crystals glowed with a blueish-white light as the tips of each pyramid came closer to touching. The sound increased in volume and the crystals became brighter. When the points finally touched, the light was so intense that it hurt to look directly at it. Everyone put on their tinted glasses and watched the demonstration with growing awe. After thirty seconds, the sound decreased and then stopped altogether. The audience sat in awed silence as the light softened back to a comfortable glow. Mark walked back to the pedestal and removed the crystals from the mounts holding them at their bases. He then turned and handed them back to the President.

Matt saw that the two crystals were now fused together. The way they melded together looked almost like an odd hour glass when viewed from the side. However, the offset bases did indeed create a six-pointed star that could be seen from several angles as he rotated it in his hands. He asked, "Those tablets in Giza told you how to do this?"

Nuri replied, "Not directly, but we learned a great deal about resonant frequencies that science had not understood before now. It is through the proper application of sound vibration that quasi-chemical reactions with solid objects, like these crystals, become possible."

"But what does that have to do with unlimited energy?" Matt sounded confused and was feeling a little overwhelmed by what he'd just witnessed.

"Mr. President," Mark began, "it will be easier to show you first and then explain what you're seeing." And with that he placed the crystal back on top of the pedestal.

Nuri activated the low note sound again while Mark hit another switch on the pedestal. The spectators gasped when the pedestal started to descend into the floor but the crystal held its position as if floating in midair. Nuri and Mark then produced a number of common electronic devices and placed them on the two folding tables sitting in front of the spectators. The devices were then plugged into a power strip which was not plugged into anything. The gadgets included a cell phone, a microwave oven, a hair dryer, and a laptop computer. A portable window air conditioner was then wheeled in alongside the other devices and it too was plugged into the power strip.

Nuri stepped back to his console and the sound changed. The "oh" sound gracefully rose one octave at a time until it was too high to be heard by the human ear. Suddenly, a light beam shot up from the floor below into the crystal. That beam refracted out as a separate ray linking the crystal to the power strip connected to the devices on the tables. Each of the electronics came to life the instant the beam of light hit the power strip. The displays on the cell phone and laptop showed they were booting up. The hair dryer moved as it started blowing hot air and the microwave oven flashed 12:00 am in the LED display. Even the AC unit began blowing air which became cool just moments later.

Matt was no electrician, but he knew the circuit breaker should have blown with all the juice being drawn through the power strip. He walked over to the tables for a better look. That the power strip itself was not plugged into an electrical socket left him dumbfounded. Upon closer inspection, Matt saw that a tiny crystal was attached to the plug end of the power strip.

Mark then picked up the cell phone and unplugged it. The display went black as the power had obviously been cut. He asked Matt to open the back of the cell phone. It was no surprise that the battery had already been removed. However, Mark took a moment to install a tiny crystal into the cell phone that looked similar to the one on the power strip. The cell phone came back to life.

Matt now saw that a separate light beam went directly to the cell phone from the main crystal. It followed the phone as Matt moved it around and the power remained on. He then ran his hand through the new light beam. Nothing changed with the phone and he felt no effect on his hand. It was clear they had discovered how to transmit electrical energy without wires or other physical means of transference.

"We can see the beams of light only because we infused this lab with particles that make them visible. Otherwise, we'd see no signs of the energy passing between the crystal and these electronic units," Mark explained.

"This is incredible!" said Matt. "But where does the power come from originally to cause all this?"

Nuri fielded the question. "That's why we wanted you to see what it did first. The answer is hard to believe unless you've observed it in action beforehand."

Mark jumped in, "We've learned that the earth acts as a capacitor for the energy produced by the Sun. When the right resonant frequency is applied and this crystal conduit is available, it greatly increases the power strip's capacity. Any electrical device with a receiving crystal can operate through a wireless connection to the main crystal. Also, connecting a receiving crystal to the main breaker in an electrical panel will power any hard-wired devices that are connected to it. We have yet to find a limit to the amount of power the main crystal can provide to any number of receivers."

Nuri added, "This technology brings a whole new meaning to the term 'precious stones.' The receiving crystal functions like a power regulator or director for the energy it attracts. They automatically draw the exact amount of power needed for the optimal function of each device connected to it."

"You mean that beam coming up from the ground is actually stored energy from the earth guided by the crystal to run these electronics?" Matt was beginning to see what they meant, but he hadn't a clue how it worked. He also took a step back from the main beam just to be careful.

Nuri said, "Yes, you have the idea. And before you ask, we still don't know very much about why it works. However, we can't find any negative effects on living tissue or inert substances regardless of how we have measured it. If anything, we think this technology has great potential for healing living tissue. The uses for this technology are probably limitless."

The President said in a commanding voice, "Ladies and gentlemen, can I have the room for about ten minutes with Doctors Heston and Zayd?"

Everyone filed out leaving Matt, Mark and Nuri alone except for the two agents standing by the door out of earshot. The President stood still for a moment, deep in thought.

Matt finally turned to Mark and Nuri, "I hadn't heard anything about the healing potential you just spoke of with this technology. What makes you think resonant frequency energy has the capability to heal?"

Nuri answered, "We only just figured this out ourselves! Jason, the soldier inside the chamber with us, must have activated some sort of healing therapy when he touched the pedestal that also started the resonant frequency generator. There were so many distractions in the chamber that night that it was easy to overlook. Our working theory was discovered after a close examination of the video Mark inadvertently recorded in the chamber. The recording showed us that Jason had been visibly scanned with some sort of green light. That is what led us to surmise it also healed him in the process. Mark too was affected, but neither Jason nor Mark was certain they had been healed until they underwent physicals to confirm the changes."

Matt asked, "You say they were healed in the chamber, but the soldier had to be in top shape or he wouldn't have been assigned to the Delta

Force team. And what was wrong with Mark that a healing couldn't be attributed to something else?"

Mark smiled, "I had type 1 diabetes since I was diagnosed at the age of ten. My pancreas and insulin levels have apparently been nominal since I left the chamber."

"Well, that is impressive, but the soldier couldn't have had any serious medical issues. Right?" Matt asked.

Nuri responded, "His case is even more of a mystery. At first, the doctor was not surprised that he was perfectly healthy. Then he saw in the soldier's medical history that he had had his gall bladder removed about five years ago. The MRI revealed it had grown back and was functioning perfectly. The tests also revealed that a broken bone in his right leg that mended long ago appears now to have never been injured."

Mark added, "It seems likely that healing is a part of the pedestals' design. Nuri didn't touch the pedestals and nothing changed in his physical condition. We're still deciphering the information contained on the 32 tablets, but so far we haven't discovered how to channel resonant frequency power toward healing."

"Is that a secret that is now lost to the world because that chamber under the Sphinx was destroyed?" Matt asked.

Nuri sighed, "Perhaps, but there is hope it might still be found. The Hall of Records in Egypt is rumored to have been one of three in existence. The other two are still hidden but may yet be located. Once we have learned all we can from the discovery in Egypt, we intend to return to archeology to search for one or both of the remaining chambers like we found in Egypt."

"I have a favor to ask of you," Matt began. "I need the two of you to accompany me to a special meeting of the heads of state at the United Nations. I want you to show them what you have just shown me. I intend to offer them access to this new form of electrical energy. Please continue to maintain strict confidentiality regarding any of these discoveries to the press or anyone else not already part of your team here at JPL."

They both readily agreed.

Matt had a second request. "I'm intrigued by the idea that there might be other hidden places in the world containing similar technology to what was destroyed in Egypt. Assuming you believe that is possible, how quickly can you begin to search for them?"

Mark and Nuri were pleased that their sabbatical was about to be extended for an indefinite period.

Chapter 30

Later that same day, Matt and Erin were in the Executive Suite of Air Force One returning to Washington. This was the first Erin had been alone with Matt since his meeting with Mark and Nuri at JPL. He brought her up to date on what he had witnessed there and the incredible potential for resonant frequency power.

"So we will soon have the ability to generate unlimited electrical power and send it wirelessly to any point in the world. The cost of providing this power is practically zero compared to fossil fuels or even sustainable energy alternatives. The United States could soon be the sole supplier of all the world's power needs from one location," Matt said excitedly.

"But won't that bankrupt our own energy corporations? How many people will this new technology put on the unemployment lines?" Erin said with genuine concern.

"I've thought of that, too. Those are just two of the points that need to be addressed. As part of the answer, I intend to nationalize "RFP" technology for several reasons. First, the corporations that will be financially harmed by this discovery should be bought out by the nationalized resonant power company at their current market values. Second, those people who lose their jobs in this process should be retrained to facilitate bringing this new technology to the world," Matt offered.

"But to nationalize the energy industry so that it is owned and operated by our government goes against the free enterprise system. Why would you decide to do that?" Erin asked.

"Actually, public utilities in this country are often run as a controlled monopoly. In the case of our water supply, the government is most often the owner and operator. It's done that way to ensure the public safety and to promote efficiency. But the proper handling of RFP can accomplish far more than just that," Matt said with a nod.

"What exactly do you have in mind?" Erin could tell he was leading up to something they had not discussed before.

He said with a smile, "Resonant frequency power is such an improvement over fossil fuels that it will inevitably be used throughout the world. Nationalizing the revenues of the international energy industry means all the profits would go to the government. This windfall could easily do away with the need for federal taxes. It is possible that all government functions could be funded from RFP doing away with taxes in this country altogether. If other countries want to nationalize their power industry in the same way, they too could lower or eliminate the need for taxes. As long as any sovereign nation abides by our rules for maintaining a peaceful coexistence, we will provide unlimited RFP to them at a reasonable cost.

Erin's mind raced through all the implications of what Matt just said. "Here's a technical question I've wanted to ask. How would they measure the amount of power each country consumes through the crystals to know how much to bill them?"

"The brains at JPL figured that one out," Matt explained. "The receptor crystals that draw the power can be tuned to different frequencies. They say it's a lot like keeping cell phone accounts separated. Each country will have its own frequency and sub-frequencies so that the power consumed can be divided and measured down to a single customer. Because the technology appears to work across any distance and through any barrier, there won't be a place on earth where power won't be available to those who subscribe."

"But is this technology safe?" she asked, trying to find the flaws in Matt's plan.

"It appears to be far safer than what we have now. The receptor crystals only draw the amount of power needed to operate each end-use of the power. Tests show that if a person inadvertently touches a dangerous electrical connection, the power automatically ceases at that point until the connection with living tissue is broken," Matt said, still impressed with the many implications of this discovery.

"But won't the people of other nations try to duplicate or circumvent the system? Can't they reverse engineer this technology to bypass our monopoly on this type of energy?" Erin asked.

Matt answered, "From what I'm told, without the knowledge gained from those 32 tablets, we could have gone for centuries without learning of resonant frequency technology. Yes, eventually everyone will be able to duplicate it, but how much better will the world be by then?"

He was still wrestling with an ethical dilemma he had yet to work out. Matt asked Erin what she thought. "Do you think I have the right to claim U.S. ownership of this technology that was discovered under the Sphinx in Egypt?"

Erin smiled, appreciating that Matt was concerned over this point. "Except for those first two crystals the soldier took with him, the property that legally belongs to Egypt is still there under tons of earth. Give the original crystal pieces back to the Egyptian government and the law has been fulfilled."

Matt marveled at how quickly she came up with the perfect solution to a problem he'd been struggling through for days. He decided to ask about the other ethical considerations. "Do you think it's fair to withhold RFP energy from countries that violate the peace plan?"

Erin was quick to respond, "Yes. They don't have to buy power from the United States if they don't abide by the conditions that go along with our offer to provide them with safe, inexpensive, reliable power in unlimited quantities. That does bring up the question of what happens when you are no longer in charge. The world leaders may trust that Matthew Alexander will always be fair, but what about your successors?"

He smiled as he said, "If I have learned anything through all of this, it is that each nation elects or inherits the leadership it deserves. If we continue to work together for the good of all, then the right people will be elected when it's time for me to step down."

Erin suddenly remembered, "You never did tell me what happened with Generals McComb and Newman. What exactly did they do that compelled you to ask for their resignations?"

Matt replied thoughtfully, "They were no longer the right people for those positions. I would have fired George Salazar, but he disappeared. Simply said, it was clear to me that they were all working against the peace plan instead of helping it to succeed. The moment they became more of a liability to our nation's interests than an asset, I asked them to resign."

After they touched down at Andrews Air Force base, Erin asked a last question before they faced the reporters on the tarmac. "Is everything that was left behind in that Egyptian chamber lost forever?"

Matt smiled as he considered her question. "Those two archeologists, Mark and Nuri, are convinced there are two other hidden locations like the one they found under the Sphinx. My hope is that they will eventually track down one or both of them. And I plan to do all I can to help them succeed!"

★★★

Mark started reading a government white paper on resonant frequency power knowing it would be a sure cure for his insomnia. He was dozing off before he got to the second page but found he was still consciously aware of his thoughts. He recognized that he was dreaming and tried to remember what this state was called. The term popped into his mind. He was experiencing a lucid dream.

As he took in his surroundings, he tried to identify the people in the room with him. He locked eyes with Nuri but his friend stared blankly back at him without recognition. Mark couldn't remember seeing the other three people before. While they looked human in appearance, they seemed to consist more of white light than flesh and blood.

The brightest light of the three spoke first, "There is no reason to be afraid. No harm will come to you here. I am Amelius. This is Ariel and Halaliel," he said as he pointed to his companions. "We are gathered here with the two of you to discuss your future."

Nuri suddenly came out of his trance and asked, "Are you some sort of angels like in the Qur'an or the Bible?"

Halaliel answered, "As your subconscious mind takes greater control, you will soon remember the answer, but it is both yes and no. Yes, in that

Ariel and I are angels, as you define such things. No, because Amelius is a soul like yourselves."

Mark interrupted him by asking, "What's the difference between an angel and a soul?"

Ariel responded, "There is almost no difference when a soul is making cooperative choices where everyone gains. Angels only make choices that are intended to benefit all. Ideally, souls do the same, but unlike angels, they can make selfish choices where they sometimes try to take advantage of others."

Nuri blurted out, "But what about Lucifer? Wasn't he an angel?"

Amelius smiled and said, "No. Lucifer is a soul. As Ariel said, there is little difference between souls and angels when all choices are made in harmony. With Lucifer's first selfish thought, the difference became clear. But we are here specifically to help you choose what is to come next in your earthly lives."

Mark asked, "Why? What makes us so special? I find it hard to believe you meet with everyone like this to discuss their future, or do you?"

It was Ariel who answered, "Make no mistake in understanding that you are indeed special. The same is true of every soul in existence. However, your recent choices, along with those of many others, have moved both of you into a unique position. You can make a difference by helping to shape a wonderful future for humankind."

Nuri was skeptical. "I admit that we're in the limelight at the moment because of resonant frequency power and discovering the Hall of records in Egypt, but that will soon pass. We plan to return to archeology just as soon as we can."

Halaliel laughed, That much is certain! But the choice that lies before you is which long-lost discoveries you will pursue, if any. You will find that you are not so welcome in Egypt after the destruction of their great treasures. The Egyptian government will soon connect your quick exit from Cairo to the discovery of resonant frequency power from underneath the Sphinx. That you decided to share this remarkable discovery with the United States rather than Egypt will present an interesting array of choices in response to President Alexander's pending plans.

Mark sadly saw where this would lead. "Archeologists don't really function well with fame or infamy. What options do we have left that don't completely change our lives and careers?"

Amelius adopted a consoling tone, "To use a cliché from earth, 'That ship has already sailed.' Your lives will never be the same as before, but see what possibilities are ahead for you that have only recently become available!"

Mark and Nuri watched as their surroundings became a 3-D experience where they could see all the consequences of their possible future choices. The wonders they could yet discover would not come without great risk. They also saw potentially deadly challenges already developing that would reveal themselves once President Alexander was no longer in office.

They were shown that their discoveries in Egypt would not bring lasting peace to the world. They saw that many people were already planning to undermine the technological gift of resonant frequency power. The world's toughest challenges still lay ahead and Mark and Nuri would be at the center of the global conflict. They could also choose to stay out of the fray and live comfortable lives without risk if they would give up their careers in archeology.

The future scenarios faded away and Amelius came back into their view. "Now you understand the choices that are before you at this critical point in humanity's timeline. You have the potential to achieve your own goals as well as help the souls of earth to become better people. You can also choose to 'let this cup pass' if that is your will. No one is forcing you to take the more difficult path. If you decide not to serve in this manner, others will eventually step up to fulfill this important role."

Mark and Nuri suddenly realized they could read each other's thoughts. Neither was particularly spiritual or altruistic, but they both doggedly pursued the truth regardless of where that led. They silently agreed that they were two of the most unlikely and reluctant heroes ever. It was simply by chance that what they wanted to do most also fell in line with the greatest results that they had just been shown.

They looked at the three glowing beings and the light emanating from them became even brighter as the shapes before them vanished. Both Mark and Nuri heard them say together, "You have chosen well and the world will benefit because of this. You will feel moments of regret over this decision, but if you persevere in being of service to all, you cannot fail. In times of fear or doubt, remember these words of encouragement: When you find yourself walking through the valley of death, there is nothing to fear, for all that is good is always with you!"

To be continued...

The author of *Through the Valley of Death: Armageddon*, John Schroeder, was 45 years old when he wrote his first book. He was a natural entrepreneur and started his first company at 23. His writing skills were initially geared toward selling products and services rather than trying to educate and entertain. Along the way John married, earned a BBA in Finance, an MBA in Marketing, a First Class Radiotelephone FCC license, was promoted to Captain in the U.S. Army Reserve, ordained as a non-denominational minister, and became a member of Mensa. His interest in science and academics shifted when he discovered the World Wide Web in the 1990s. That was when chat rooms became popular on the internet.

John began discussing and debating a variety of topics by exchanging thousands of written posts with others who had similar interests online. Those digital exchanges became the basis for John's first book in 1999. *God in a Chat Room*, now out of print, presented a compilation of internet discussions John had over the years. He explored many intriguing and controversial subjects about life, science and spirituality.

John's next book, *The Price of Prosperity*, was published in 2003. It is a self-help guide that examines the laws of prosperity and features John's personal experiences as he applied those concepts in his own life.

In 2012, John's writing went in a new direction with the intention of reaching a wider readership. Using a Q&A format, the book *Let Not Your Heart Be Troubled* offers an uplifting and positive perspective of life. The heartfelt and humorous conversations assert that we live in a friendly, childproof universe.

While all of John's books have been well received, he had long desired to write a fictional novel based on the spiritual concepts detailed in his other publications. During lunch one afternoon with his wife, Stephanie, John envisioned the theme for such a book. Stephanie took notes as John created a fantastic, yet plausible, scenario for an optimistic future made possible with the discovery of sophisticated technology. That idea grew into more than just one book. This novel marks the first adventure in a trilogy that blends fact, fiction and spirituality into an intriguing story and world view of better days to come.

John is now retired and devotes his time to his wife, his furry canine children, public speaking, writing books and articles as well as playing sports and hiking the local mountains near his home in Scottsdale, Arizona.